Praise for *Blessed in The Detours of Life – a collection of personal Psalms.*

The Psalms were initially titled "Tehillim," which in Hebrew means "praise songs." The book of Psalms in the Bible is a compilation of composite works of lyrical poems composed by several writers, with many attributed to King David.

Following the tradition of the Psalmist of the old, we are fortunate to have a contemporary representation of the Twenty-Third Psalm and others undertaken by the HBI students under the direction of their Instructor, Pamela Rasheed, titled *"Blessed In The Detours Of Life – a collection of personal psalms."*

Pastor Subash Cherian
Senior Pastor of The Highland Church, New York

There are numerous streams of truth running through the scriptures, and nowhere is this more evident than in the personal, poetic, and prophetic flows found in the Psalms. I pray that all who read and meditate on the Psalms in the scriptures and this collection of personal Psalms by today's followers of Jesus Christ will receive illumination and comfort from these intimate and personal expressions of God's love, providence, goodness, and faithfulness.

Collin Baker
Highland Bible Institute

I must commend the authors for the effort and initiative in putting these wonderful pieces together. The main idea behind the creation of this book is unique and every personal experience shared in the book is touching and inspirational. Above all, the exhortations at the end of every buildup story are loaded, and full of insights and wisdom. I'm personally blessed while reading through them. This book will embolden more people to face life while trusting in God.

Celeste Ava, Editor, Fiverr

Co-Authors

Rev. Brenda Collier, Evangelist Ida Humphrey, Chaplain., Dr. Cheryl James,

Edith Revell, Joyann Jagdeo, Lavonne Jackson-Wright,

Kathleen Smith, Patricia White, Elvira Alexander, Karen Perez,

Geraldine Simmons, Cavelle Francis, and Roshini Balgobin,.

July 17, 2023

To Lisa My Elijah

Blessed In The Detours Of Life

A Collection of Personal Psalms

Written By the Instructor and Students of

The Highland Church Bible Institute

May God order your steps & don't let detours of life stop you

Pamela G. Rasheed

Blessed In The Detours Of Life −
a collection of personal Psalms

Copyright 2023 by Pamela Rasheed

Editorial support by: Celeste_ava/fiverr
Layout by: Aalishaa/fiverr
Cover Design by: Sam_4321/fiverr

Except as printed under the United States Copyright Act of 1976, no parts of this book may be reproduced or distributed in any form or by any means or stored in a database or retrieval system, without the prior written permission of the author. If you would like to quote from or otherwise use materials from this book, please contact the author at pamela1992@gmail.com

Table of Content

Forward – Pastor Subash Cherian vii
Preface ix
Introduction 1
HBI Director's Note – Collin Baker 5
Acknowledgment 6
Instructor's Note – Pamela Rasheed 8

Chapters
1. God's Response to Prayer - Edith Revell 12
2. A Mother's Grief At The Loss of Her
   Children - Elvira Alexander........................... 21
3. God's Rescue of a Backslider - Pamela Rasheed 30
4. God's Provision After the Last Drop
   - Cavelle Francis 43
5. Utterances of Women In The Bible That
   Are Psalm-like – Rev. Brenda Collier............ 49
6. A Psalm of Remembrance –
   Chaplain Dr. Cheryl Y. James 65
7. Hearing the Voice of God - Geraldine Simmons 79
8. God's Provision and Direction - Lavonne Jackson - 85
9. God's Divine Healing - Joyann Jagdeo............ 93
10. Who God Is To Us – Chaplain, Dr. Cheryl James. 101
11. Longing And Waiting For A Child - Karen Perez ... 105
12. Refuge in Christ After Losing A Son -
    Evangelist Ida Mack-Humphrey 111
13. The Amazement at God's Faithfulness
    - Pamela Rasheed 118
14. Deliverance from The Snare - Kathleen Smith...... 134

15. A Call to Praise and Worship
    −Evangelist Ida Humphrey 142
16. Jesus Said "Child, You Have to Wait"
    - Reverend Brenda Collier 159
17. God's Power in Deliverance - Patricia White 171
18. God's Love and Comfort in Rejection
    - Roshini Balgobin 177

Foreword

The Psalms were initially titled "Tehillim," which in Hebrew means "praise songs." The book of Psalms in the Bible is a compilation of composite works of lyrical poems composed by several writers, with many attributed to King David.

Psalm 23, often attributed to King David, is considered one of the most exquisite and captivating poems ever written, and this is a passage like the other Psalms where people had always gone when they were hurting or engulfed with fear and anxiety.

This is even truer during the present crises, where so many fear the future and are anxious about what will happen. This also has been a moment when so many people have turned to The Psalms in the Bible for comfort, strength, and solace. There was also a time during the pandemic when the study of The Psalms was one of the courses offered in a two-semester study at the Highland Bible Institute (HBI) in 2022.

Following the tradition of the Psalmist of the old, we are fortunate to have a contemporary representation of the Twenty-Third Psalm and others undertaken by the HBI students under the direction of their Instructor,

Pamela Rasheed, titled *"Blessed In The Detours Of Life – a collection of personal psalms."*

And like the Psalmist, they use poetic devices such as imagery, metaphors, similes, personification, and hyperbole to bring out 21st-century psalms based on their personal life experiences. Life and its vicissitude continue to happen to all of us in unimaginable ways, as in the old times. Yet, the Word of God remains true to strengthen the foundation of our very existence until the end of times.

I commend both Sister Pamela Rasheed, her assistant instructor, Sister Ramona Deffendorf, and all the students who helped in this blessed endeavor, and I hope you enjoy a great reading experience enriching your confident trust and love for the Shepherd, our Lord Jesus Christ who carries you through the Detours Of Your own Life

Pastor Subash Cherian

Senior Pastor of The Highland Church, New York

Preface

The Psalms in this book are written by the instructor and students at the Highland Avenue Church's Bible Institute in Jamaica, Queens, New York. It is a product of a two-semester study on the Book of Psalms in 2022.

At the end of a basic study of Psalms in the Spring 2022 semester, one of the students, Reverend Brenda Collier, suggested that the students write their own psalms based on their personal life experiences. She had done a similar assignment several years ago when she initially studied The Psalms. So, during the Summer 2022 break, I was impressed by the Holy Spirit to not only continue the studies of the Psalms but to challenge the students to write their own Psalms and the backstories from which their Psalms were inspired.

Most of the students registered again for Psalm part two in the Autumn of 2022. I was led to take a different approach to the structure of the lessons, where we would examine the depth of human emotions from which the Psalms in the Bible were written. As we explored major categories of the Psalms and examined the various life experiences that triggered the many aspects of human emotions, it was evident that we, too have, at some point or another faced similar and sometimes parallel circumstances where we have also uttered our own Psalms.

I was further impressed to have these Psalms published in a book that will encourage and uplift others. The students became excited with this course challenge that successfully led to this book: *Blessed In The Detours of Life – a collection of personal Psalms*.

On countless occasions, and unbeknownst to us, we have expressed joy, happiness, anguish, fear, praise, prayers, worship, thanksgiving, lamentation, uncertainties, doubts, imprecations, pondering and questioning our despondencies that mirror those in the Holy Bible. At times, our words are uttered in inner silence and quiet pondering; other times, they are outbursts of emotions that resonate with our feelings and thoughts. We are humans full of expressions.

> *Hosea 14:2 says:*
> *Take words with you.*
> *And return to the LORD.*
> *Say to Him,*
> *"Take away all iniquity.*
> *Receive us graciously,*
> *For we will offer the sacrifices of our lips".*

As the students revisited a time in their life's events and recollected the memories of significant experiences that caused them to express to God with various emotions, they have each written a psalm and its backstory. Their personal psalms were very reflective of detours in the lives of believers who, because of their faith and trust in God, were able to be redirected with inner peace to their destiny in Him.

As the author and co-authors (instructor and students) penned their psalms and backstories, they realized that amidst uncertainty and fear, they looked to God for direction and learned to trust Him for the expected end. They learned of patience, love, contentment, and gratitude and grew in grace, wisdom, and strength. These blessings are forever life-changing, and their psalms in their detours are unto the Lord with the hope that they bless every reader.

My prayer and hope for every reader of these Psalms is that you will be challenged and encouraged to put your expressions into written words, whether high or low, in quiet pondering, prayers, praises, and worship to our creator for the process of doing so, with God in the center, can bring healing to the soul.

Pamela Rasheed

Introduction

What is a Detour?

A detour is an alternate route to get to a planned destination. A detour can be taken out of our own free will as a shortcut or to avoid a perceived setback, delay, or danger. Some detours are placed by others to accomplish their own plan and purpose but sometimes force us to figure out a roundabout to our destination. There are instances when detours are unavoidable, mainly because they are the only alternate route to get you moving forward at the time. Many times, detours would take you by surprise, bringing uncertainty, fear, frustration, and anxiety. On the other hand, some detours are taken on a whim and out of leisure just to see or embark on an unplanned adventure. In some instances, detours can get you lost or confused, that then cause you to have to figure yet another way out.

The Psalms in this book in no way replace or adds to God-inspired Word, the Holy Bible, but they are the ongoing and never-ending human expressions as they seek God amidst life's ups and downs of life.

The authors of the Psalms in the Holy Bible have put many human experiences and emotional, spiritual, and psychological expressions into words for us. David is not the only one who wrote the book of Psalms in the Bible, but others, including Moses, whose words were uttered in Psalm 90, Solomon, the sons of Korah, and others whose names are not mentioned (orphan Psalms), and as we studied them, we concluded that only God could turn upside-down into right-side-up, emptiness into fulfillment, confusion into understanding, and brokenness into beautiful vessels.

An example of King David's failure and brokenness expressed in Psalm 51 teaches about the state of the many conflicting emotions that were wrapped up in his one life's event, a major detour he willfully took by staying at his home and leisurely walking on his balcony while his soldiers went to battle. Most of us are aware of his fleshly desire for Bathsheba that night and his eventual sin with her despite being aware she was someone else's wife. Some of us may be aware of his attempts to conceal his failure and her pregnancy, including his plot that resulted in the death of her husband, Uriah. But just when King David, the man after God's own heart (1 Samuel 13:14; Acts 13:22), thought that his plan had worked, his sin was well covered-up, and he was almost applauded for being noble in taking in the wife of his fallen soldier, Nathan the prophet paid him a visit to confront him with his sin as God had instructed. As king, David certainly had the power to do worse; perhaps banish the prophet, or worse, but instead, he owned up to his sins and repented.

A few things David said amid all of what he felt emotionally, physically, and psychologically are: "Have mercy upon me," "Deliver me from the guilt of bloodshed, "Do not cast me away from Your presence," "Do not take thy Holy Spirit away from me" and much more. Imagine the sheer guilt, fear, anguish, grief, humility, and shame. He loves the Lord, but he knows that he caused God grief, but even as King, he also knew that he needed God's forgiveness and Love yet again.

We are all like David, weak and in need of God's strength along this pilgrim journey, from our birth in Christ to our ultimate home-going to God. Our intention is to go from being born-again to paradise, but the journey is filled with detours, and we become aware that we are nothing without His grace and guidance along the way. We come to know that God is after our hearts, after all. When He allows us to go through situations, He is teaching us to seek Him and conditioning us to trust Him. As we take His lead, we can watch Him bring us through. God wants our hearts, and he chastens us because he loves us.

Hebrews 26:6,7 says:
For whom the LORD loves, He chastens,
And scourges every son whom He receives."
If you endure chastening,
God deals with you as with sons;
for what son is there whom a father does not chasten?

There is a famous saying: "you can run, but you cannot hide." We see the story of Jonah, who attempted to run away from God's plan. His detour was in the belly of a whale, and he needed to be rescued by God and redirected to fulfill His will (Jonah 1:1-17).

Jesus is our perfect example of when a detour can lead to a blessing for us and others (The Gospel of John, chapter 4). Although the path from Judea to Galilee was shorter through Samaria, Jews avoided it because they disliked and distrusted the Samaritans. But, Jesus, on his way to Galilee from Judea, took that unusual route where He met the Samaritan woman, and her life was never the same.

While on earth, Jesus faced every human emotion, challenge, and temptation possible, many of which we have not faced, and yet he overcame them all and imparted life to any who would come unto Him. He shows us that with God, we too can overcome and be a blessing to others, even in our detours.

Pamela Rasheed

Note from the Dean of Highland Bible Institute

There are numerous streams of truth running through the scriptures, and nowhere is this more evident than in the personal, poetic, and prophetic flows found in the Psalms. In this collection of personal Psalms - *Blessed in the Detours of Life* – each student and their instructor provided testimony about the unexpected and sometimes painful twists and turns of life that culminate with a celebration of God's sovereign presence and guidance throughout their journey.

I am overjoyed by the boldness, unity, and dedication of this HBI class for stepping out in obedience in undertaking this project.

I pray that all who read and meditate on the Psalms in the scriptures and this collection of personal Psalms by today's followers of Jesus Christ will receive illumination and comfort from these intimate and personal expressions of God's love, providence, goodness, and faithfulness.

Collin Baker
Highland Bible Institute.

Acknowledgment

This book would not be possible without the help and guidance of the Holy Spirit, and I must say Thank You, Father, Son, and Holy Spirit, for being with me.

I am grateful to all the co-authors who were students in the two-semester study of the Psalms and have contributed their backstories and personal psalms that made this book possible. These wonderful ladies are Edith Revell, Joyann Jagdeo, Lavonne Jackson-Wright, Kathleen Smith, Patricia White, Elvira Alexander, Karen Perez, Geraldine Simmons, Cavelle Francis, Roshini Balgobin, Rev. Brenda Collier, Evangelist Ida Humphrey, and Chaplain., Dr. Cheryl James.

A special thank you to Sister Ramona Deffendorf for assisting me in teaching this class and encouraging each of us with the courses.

I am very grateful to Reverend Brenda Collier, fellow HBI instructor, Evangelist Ida Humphrey, and Chaplain., Dr. Cheryl James for their help in the planning phase, their contribution to the three special non-psalm chapters, assisting with the exhortations at the end of each Psalm, and their continued prayers and constant encouragement throughout the process.

A heartfelt thank you to our senior Pastor, Subash Cherian. Pastor Andre Hantz, and Brother Collin Baker for their prayers and encouragement and for trusting us with the publication of this book. Special appreciation to the leadership and staff of the Highland church who, behind the scenes, have tirelessly supported the Bible Institute in all that gets done every semester.

Instructor's note

The Bible's twenty-third Psalm, written by King David, is one of the most beautiful poetries of all time, recited by Christians and non-Christians alike in times of sickness, sorrow, and need for reassurance.

In the first four verses of this Psalm, But, as king, David recalls his relationship with his flock when he was just a shepherd boy. He reflected upon the role of the shepherd in ensuring the protection, provision, restoration, and safety of his flock.

King David beautifully weaved the importance of the rod and staff in this psalm because they were important tools needed to keep and protect the sheep from the attacks of the enemy and realign them back onto the path of righteousness.

The LORD is my shepherd; I shall not want.
² He maketh me to lie down in green pastures:
he leadeth me beside the still waters.
³ He restoreth my soul:
he leadeth me in the paths of righteousness for his name's sake.
⁴ Yea, though I walk through the valley of the shadow of death,
I will fear no evil: for thou art with me;
thy rod and thy staff they comfort me.

When a sheep wandered off, the shepherd would use the hook on his staff to draw it back and realign it into the proper path. And when an enemy came to attack the sheep, the shepherd used the rod to defend the sheep. Therefore, the rod and staff in this Psalm were used to protect and realign the sheep in their detour. If it weren't for the shepherd's love for his sheep and his rod and staff, many sheep would be lost during their wandering and detours. The shepherd's love for their flock ensures they do whatever it takes to protect and guide them back to safety.

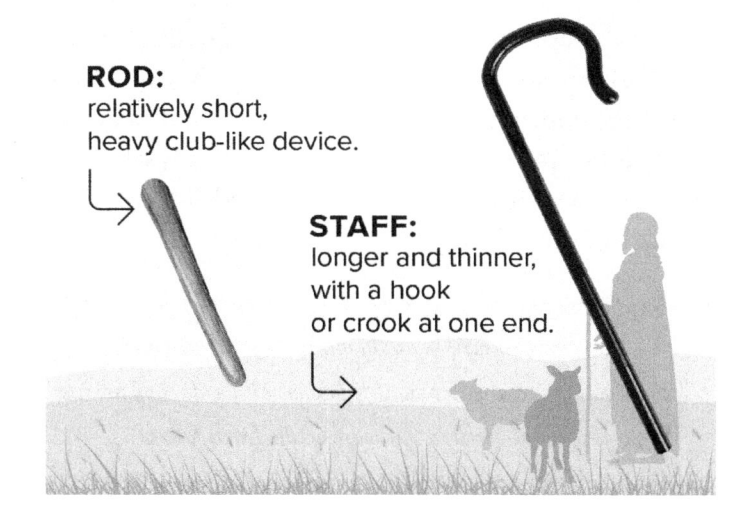

ROD:
relatively short, heavy club-like device.

STAFF:
longer and thinner, with a hook or crook at one end.

King David puts himself in the position of the sheep in verses one through four. He mused on the beauty of being a recipient of protection, provision, and restoration while in the presence of the great shepherd, Jesus.

Life is beautiful when everything is going right. We are filled with bliss while enjoying mountain-top-like experiences, but when we face those low valley experiences and feel lost and depressed, life is more rewarding if Almighty God, Jesus, and the Holy Spirit are with us. Let God's navigational system (GPS), which includes the rod and the staff mentioned in Psalm 23, defend and realign you to His purpose in the valleys and the detours of your lives. Let it comfort, redirect, and never leave you vulnerable. Our life's journey is not only beautiful but peaceful, rewarding, and fulfilling, and these are just a few treasures we find when we are plugged into the GPS in the detours of our lives.

⁵ Thou preparest a table before me in the presence of mine enemies: thou anointest my head with oil; my cup runneth over.
⁶ Surely goodness and mercy shall follow me all the days of my life: and I will dwell in the house of the LORD forever.

King David was used to preparing lavish banquets for many guests where he showered them with delicious foods, wines, and gifts. He made his guests feel welcome and very special.

In the latter two verses of this exquiaite F
puts himself in the position of the a favored
mused on the beauty of being in the awesome
of the Great King, and a recipient at a lavish banquet
prepared just for him.

Oil speaks of anointing and hospitality. In the old times, when a guest entered a home, the host showed hospitaility by anointing the head of the guest. Here, David, a guest, expressed how highy favored he is to his host, The King - Jesus. He said "thou anointest my head with oil, and my cup runneth over".

We are highly Favored!

Pamela Rasheed

CHAPTER 1
EDITH REVELL

THE STORY BEHIND THIS PSALM

A personal plea to God for mercy during a difficult time

When I was in my teens, we moved to Puerto Rico. Some of my cousins that lived there were Pentecostal. They were always witnessing to me, but I never gave my heart to the Lord. I heard them sing and pray next door once a week. I read my Biblebecause I loved the book of Proverbs. So, I knew there was a God, but I did not have a personal relationship with Him. I moved on with life.

My father was abusive towards my mother for years, but I knew it was the alcohol he drank that changed his personality. He was a functioning alcoholic. My family did not lack anything except peace. When we moved to Puerto Rico, my father and mother opened a business. They sold everything you'd find at Walgreens except food and prescription drugs. My father purchased a van and filled it up with merchandise to sell in different parts of our town. People would wait for him to come by during the weekends to buy what they needed. Mostly every Saturday. Despite being a successful businessman, he had a habit of drinking long, late hours with his friends after work. However, he often yelled at and subjected my mother to verbal and physical abuse upon returning home. When I heard the van arrives late at night on Saturdays, I would get down on my knees and pray to God for compassion. I remained in that position until my father took a bath, had dinner, and went to bed. During those moments, I pleaded with God to prevent my father from being abusive on that particular night.

Every Saturday night, I continued with that same routine. I would kneel, shake and cry out to God in silence. Fear paralyzed me. I was weary, tired, and beaten down. As soon as my father went to bed and I heard his bedroom door close, I would thank the Lord, my father was peaceful, and I would get up from my knees.

I kneeled and prayed every Saturday because prayer worked. It was the only thing that worked, and I was in awe. The Lord also gave me a forgiving heart, and I was able to love my earthly father and honor him. I believe this was the beginning of my walk with the Lord.

Blessed In The Detours Of Life

A Psalm of God's Response to Sincere Prayer

- Edith Revell -

Like a leaf falling,
floating,
crashing,
bruised,
clothing torn,
tired and weary.
A season in my life.

Lord, you were there, I kneeled and prayed
Weekend after weekend,
I cried out to You
Have mercy!

I did not know You, but I knew You were there.
I knew there is a God. So I was told.

A God that can move mountains.

Blessed In The Detours Of Life

Mountains I felt were unmovable.
Impossible!
Too big to manage on my own.
Who can I turn to?
I said to myself on those dark lonely weekends.
Fear paralyzed me.
There is no hope!
My heart pounded in desperation!

Then I remembered!
You still the raging waters
At Your command all storms cease.
Fear will leave, sunshine taking its place.

I cried out to You.
I want to know this peace.
I want that joy I heard about.
Come to my rescue I said kneeling by my bed,
face in my hands.

Let it be true my heart said,
You have all the power, and You do as You will.
I prayed, and I waited.

At last, I heard Your voice in the midst of my turmoil.
At last, I saw the leaves springing forth.

Edith Revell

At last, Spring is here.

I was renewed and green again,
abiding in Jesus.
Abundant life flowing through my veins,
like an olive leaf that gives hope.
You did this for me!

Author's Exhortation

When fear grips us, we feel paralyzed, not only emotionally but physically. Almost in every circumstance, fear triggers a response to either freeze, fight to maintain safety, or a flight to safety to escape the situation. It has been clinically shown that when we perceive a threat to ourselves or our loved ones, our brain sends messages to the brain to release stress hormones that help prepare us for the fight or flight response, but what about getting frozen?

More often, if we can, we may take the easy way out by fleeing the situation. Others may fight for protection, while others freeze or feel paralyzed and helpless.

I don't know if you have encountered that fear as described in Edith's situation, but I want to tell you that God is there, ready, and able to calm your fears and deliver you from harm if you would trust him. While you take deep breaths and count to three before responding, God is waiting with open arms to wrap you up and keep you safe mentally, emotionally, and physically if you would stay in God's plan or return from straying and re-commit to his divine plan for your life.

> *Surely the arm of the LORD is not too short to save,*
> *nor his ear too dull to hear.*
> *But your iniquities have separated*
> *you from your God;*
> *your sins have hidden his face from you,*
> *so that he will not hear.*
>
> *Isaiah 59:1-2 (NIV)*

Allow God to rescue you in every situation that threatens your safety in these last days. Return to the Lord, repent, and watch God calm your fears and give you reassurance.

David was running from King Saul, who wanted to kill him. He ended up in the city of Gath, a territory of the Philistine giant Goliath, whom he slayed. The leader of that city recognized David. This was a very fearful situation: running from the king who wanted him dead to end up in a city whose leader would most likely turn him over to King Saul as revenge for slaying a Philistine prior. Adding to the danger is the great resentment because David had with him Goliath's sword that he used to cut off his head.

So, fear triggers a flight response; David flew to a cave called Adullam and wrote Psalm 34 about God's protection and deliverance from fear.

*I sought the LORD, and he answered me;
he delivered me from all my fears.*

Psalm 34: 4 (NIV)

I encourage you to read Psalm 34 and the back story in 1 Samuel: 21 and 22.

Pamela Rasheed

CHAPTER 2
ELVIRA ALEXANDER

This is the back story for this psalm of Loss and Grief

On February 22, 2006, my son, Robert, passed away. He was 38 years old. He died of a massive heart attack due to an autoimmune system disorder which caused blood clots to form in his heart and right lung. The clot in his heart caused considerable damage and a very high heart rate. Robert's doctors advised him to have laser surgery to cauterize the damage, which might lower his heart rate to normal, but he could die during the procedure. His doctors also warned him that the rate at which his heart was beating would eventually result in a heart attack, which occurred two years later.

My son, Robert, was a very bright young man; he graduated from St. Lawrence College with a major degree in government and a minor in history. After graduation, he worked for Queens Justice System for a year and then decided to attend law school. He attended Ohio Northern University, Claude W. Pettit College of Law, where he earned his Juris Doctorate. After graduation, he passed the law bar exam in Georgia and practiced law in Georgia Judicial System for a few years.

Robert was a gift to the family; he was a loving son and brother to his three sisters. We miss him every day, but according to God's promises, we may meet again for all eternity.

The second reason for my psalm is the passing of my daughter, Melanie, on January 31, 2022. She left behind three children: a 33-year-old son and twin 13-year-old children, a boy and a girl.

Melanie left a legacy of care and compassion for others. She was a Certified Nursing Assistant for over thirty years. In her last position, she was the director of the facility at Second Family Social Adult Day Care Center. Because of the relationships Melanie cultivated with the registrants at Second Family, I was welcomed with open arms by all.

When covid hit, Melanie was struck by this awful virus; she became very ill, and her blood sugar levels were off the charts. Her doctors were concerned they could not control it. But by the grace of God, she lived through it. Melanie had been grappling with health problems after recovering from COVID-19. She had been experiencing constant fatigue and stomach pains for over a year. After undergoing tests, she received the news that she had Stage 4 colon cancer. This diagnosis left her devastated.

At age 55, she was told she would die, leaving her children, husband, and family. Melanie's doctors told her she might survive if she took chemotherapy treatments. The chemo worked for a few months, and then the tumors started growing again. She was given blood transfusions because the chemo was destroying her white blood cells. The chemo burned her hands and feet. Finally, her doctors told her there was nothing else they could do for her.

Despite her difficult circumstances, Melanie maintained her trust in God and held fast to her faith in Him. She believed she would be reunited with Jesus, her Lord, through His grace and mercy. God has gifted me with awesome children, and I am so grateful I had them for as long as I did.

Through grief and pain, I Bless the Lord. He is Jehovah, the God that knows the end even from the beginning, and Jesus Christ, our Lord and Savior, who gives me the strength to go on.

A Psalm of Thanksgiving Despite Grief and Loss

- Elvira Alexander -

Oh, my Father and my God,
I am consumed with pain and sorrow,
I came to you in prayer and supplication.
And ask you to save my children,
and yet they are no more.

No mother should out-live her children.
But even though they are no longer
in this earthly realm, I am grateful.
Grateful for the precious moments
we shared in love and laughter.

My Father, Jehovah,
my children trusted in you
and accepted Jesus Christ as their savior.
Praises and honor to you,
because you heard my cry of despair
and through your mercy and grace,

I am consoled, for I will see them again.

"My flesh and heart may fail,
but You God are the strength of my heart!
You are my portion forever, just like the Psalmist of old
Said in your Holy Word (Psalm 73:26).

My Father, my God,
your faithfulness surrounds me!
I am comforted by your love.
Blessed is your Holy name in all the earth forever and ever. Selah.

Co-Author's Exhortation

When we think of the course of life's natural order, it is clear that parents outliving their children is out of that order of human life. This inconceivable situation and experience can turn a person's world upside down.

The thought of losing a child is so unbearable that it can quickly turn into a devastating reality for a mother. Losing two children is a notion that is too overwhelming even to consider and can cause inconsolable heartbreak.

Losing a child permanently removes pieces of the family puzzle that cannot be replaced.

Yes, some things will not make sense to our natural mind, and the bereaved parents and loved ones are left with unanswered questions.

What can you do when you have continuously prayed for healing, and it seems God is slow to answer or does not answer at all?

What can you do when you stand on God's Word and speak every healing scripture you know, but no healing is granted?

What can you do when you haven't witnessed a physical manifestation and your decreed and stated healing hasn't worked?

What can you do when it seems like the Lord has not intervened and honored the faith prayers that bombarded heaven relentlessly?

To describe this loss as an unimaginable pain is an understatement. I am reminded of the story of Job in the Bible, who experienced a debilitating and unimaginable infirmity and, at the same time, lost all his children to physical death. I cannot imagine the depth of pain one would experience because these situations are unimaginable. But what I know for sure is that The Lord Jesus Christ loves all of us more than we can imagine. He also loves our children even more than we love them, although it may be challenging to comprehend and understand in times like this.

When we or our children leave this world as believers, a seat in God's Kingdom awaits us because the scripture states in **John 14:3** that Christ has gone ahead of us to prepare a place for us and, in the second coming, when he returns for His children, the dead in Christ will rise first to meet Him before those still here on earth. And there will be no need to pray for healing because sickness and death will have no place in God's realm. We will be whole. Every sickness, pain, infirmity, and discomfort will leave us the moment we enter God's supernatural realm because God makes everything new. **2 Corinthians 5:8** lets us know that to be absent in the body is to be present with The Lord. Physical infirmities do not exist in God's realm.

On this pilgrim journey as a believer, this fact may not lessen the pain of loss or the absence of a loved one, but the reality is that their ailments no longer exist, and the prayers of healing have been made complete in the presence of God. So, as we continue to adjust to life on earth without our loved ones, I encourage you to continue to lean on The Word of God to sustain, strengthen, and hold you up in difficult times of despair and uncertainty. The Word of God is faithful and provides many scriptures of encouragement. We may not know what tomorrow holds, but we do know who holds tomorrow.

God's promises are stated in **Psalms 34:18,** "The Lord is close to the brokenhearted and saves those who are crushed in spirit." The Good News Is; Although you may feel defeated in these situations, God is closer than you realize. He's always with you and can heal you and your broken heart. God's Word and His love can heal your heart and help you to get through anything. Matthew 11:28 tells us to "Come to me all who are weary and burdened, and I will give you rest.

The Good News Is; being brokenhearted may wear you out and deplete your strength, but casting your cares and worries before God will always give you the support you need to get through your every despair and form of distress. **Revelation: 21:4** reminds us that "He will wipe every tear from their eyes, there will be no more death or mourning or crying or pain for the old order of things has passed away." The Lord makes everything new because he is trustworthy and true. The Good News Is: You may feel alone during your time of desolation, but God's loving hand is always near. Rely on Him, and your path to healing will be made transparent and visible.

May The Lord Bless you and keep you.

May The Lord let His face shine and smile upon you and be gracious to you.

May The Lord look upon you kindly, show you His Favor and give you peace.

– Chaplain, Dr. Cheryl Y. James

CHAPTER 3

Pamela Rasheed – backstory to my Psalm

In 2012, on the 21st of July, I made the decision to visit the women's ministry at Highland Church. My goal was to explore the ministry and see if it was a good fit for me and perhaps to get back into church ministry and serve again. Having recently obtained my first nursing degree, I had been unable to attend church regularly for a few years due to my demanding schedule of work, studies, and parenting responsibilities. Moreover, the period between 2007 and 2012 was a turbulent time in my life, which resulted in me neglecting my spiritual practices, including regular prayer and reading God's Word.

I resigned from my job in 2007 as a medical assistant supervisor at an OBGYN clinic to pursue a nursing degree because, although I worked diligently to maintain the highest standard of patient care, the management was considering cutting my salary rather than increasing it due to budgeting issues. I was a mother of two (5- and 7-year-olds), and my marriage was going well. My husband approved my proposal to study full-time that year in college so I could stay focused and achieve high grades to be accepted into the very competitive nursing program. I was in my thirties with classmates who were old enough to be my kids, but that was okay as it made me feel more desperate to "not" fail. With God's help and according to plan, I successfully made the cut as a top student in the pre-clinical studies, which enabled me to be accepted immediately into the highly competitive clinical phase of the nursing program.

However, when it was evident that I was succeeding academically, issues arose in the marriage that I didn't quite understand or expect. Within a couple of years, the marriage became like a raging sea. Upon successfully completing that first year of pre-clinical, I was forced back to work in 2008 amidst growing marital tension that was escalated to boiling point by 2010. I was made aware that despite giving the impression of being supportive, my husband was secretly hoping that I would not be accepted into nursing school after all. It became clear to me later that he preferred for me to remain financially dependent on him and under his control.

In 2009-2010, during the recession under the Obama administration, my husband lost his well-paying job with no savings in the bank and his unwillingness to take a lesser-paying job. During this recession and for the first time, unemployment benefits were extended to two years, enabling my husband not to seek job opportunities. Instead, he hung out and gambled more with the online horse racing wagers. I became the main breadwinner, and his ego was apparently shattered. Our home went into foreclosure despite enough unemployment dollars to cover the mortgage and maintenance. At that time, I was a full-time employee in a management position at Columbia University Medical Center and a nursing student at night.

It shocked me when I learned that my husband was verbally and sometimes physically abusive to then our 7-year-old son because he could not tie his shoelace quickly enough to leave for school in the mornings. I got enraged and hurt when I confirmed this with my son, daughter, and babysitter. My son begged me to vow that I won't confront his dad for fear of retribution. I made that vow but had to bottle up that pain and anger. Tension soared, and our marriage was at its breaking point. I became resentful and callous due to his verbal and near-physical assault on me. I neglected my spiritual practices and stopped reading the Bible or praying. The combination of work and school left me exhausted by midnight, and the mornings always seemed to arrive too soon.

By the time of graduation in June 2012, my walk with the Lord was almost non-existent, and I was in a backslidden state. I felt like the walking dead spiritually and emotionally. I was just "going through the motion," almost like a robot. Being a private person, I masked the inner turmoil and did not reach out for help because I could not let others know that my apparent "perfect" life was a fallacy.

But thank God for Jesus who gave us a comforter, the Holy Spirit, who would teach us and lead us back to the path of righteousness (John 14:16, 26). I became self-aware that I was not in a good place, and my physical appearance seemed drained, tired, and unhappy. With this self-awareness, I decided to get up and go to the women's ministry that day just to "check things out."

On that Saturday, I was lost and spiritually dried up, yet fully masked with smiles and make-up. I sat at the back table next to the exit with the intent to leave before the session would be over or if it went too long. Before the speaker came on stage, a woman sang a song with the words: "I am not a man – I cannot lie. I am asking you to trust again… to believe again". As the lyrics struck a chord with my hardened heart, a sense of unease settled in. However, my determination to leave at the end of the song only grew stronger.

My plan did not turn out the way I orchestrated it. The speaker took the microphone and began speaking while we had our heads bowed and eyes closed. She said, "..some are in bondage right now, right here." She continued, "there is a woman here whose feet are in chains… she smiles, she raises her hand and praises the Lord, but she is in chains. Her smiles mask her burdens, and she is weighted down with chains on her feet". "Oh, my goodness!' I thought to myself. I felt she was talking about me. But how? She does not know me. This is my first time attending this gathering, and the church is enormous. "For sure," I said to myself, "she must be referring to someone else, not me." But no one else stood up, and I felt more compelled to leave this place.

I was sitting next to the exit and so desperate to leave, but the room became very quiet, and there was a stillness in the atmosphere as she continued to *describe this woman in chains.* She pleaded for the woman to stand as the Holy Spirit beckoned, but I said to myself, "*I am NOT standing. No one must know anything about me*", but I hoped that one of the other women would stand up. No one stood up, and Pride had its grip on me.

Eventually, her words over the microphone were, "The Lord is saying that this woman that He wants to minister to is sitting right in this area I am standing." I was so relieved that it wasn't me because I was by the exit, and she was on the stage. I half-opened my eyes to take a peek to ensure my assumption was accurate, but to my dismay, the speaker was standing next to me. I panicked but was still resistant. Then the Holy Spirit brought back the word of God to me:

> *Where can I go from Your Spirit?*
> *Or where can I flee from Your presence?*
> *If I ascend into heaven, You are there;*
> *If I make my bed in hell, behold, You are there.*
> *If I take the wings of the morning,*
> *And dwell in the uttermost parts of the sea,*
> *Even there, Your hand shall lead me,*
> *And Your right hand shall hold me.*
>
> *(Psalm 139: 7-12 KJV)*

The Holy Spirit reminded me of the times I longed for a breakthrough but barely spoke the audible words in prayer. But God heard my heart's non-verbal longing – He did!

At that moment, I felt busted!

I stood up; tears like a well came out of nowhere. God used the speaker to put the right words to my innermost torment. She said, "look at this heart; it is so callous, but God will peel off the scars" My sobs became louder and deeper (balling). The pride disappeared. God met me that day, and from then onwards, healing began. He has been setting my life in order, and I am in awe of who He is to me.

A PSALM WHEN I FELT BUSTED BUT BY THE POWER OF THE HOLY SPIRIT
God's Rescued a Backslider

-Pamela Rasheed-

My God and my Lord
Surely, you see me, all of me, deep within
They shone your light into
most secret places I so carefully guarded.
I did the pain even from you, who sees all
You entered in, and you rescued me.

Foolishly, I thought for certain that.
I succeeded in keeping you out
But when I could not manage on my own
you showed up and rescued me.
You are ever near, and you see me:
Through and through, all of me deep within

Like a father who keeps watch
Over his precious child
To guard her if she should falls,
and to pick her up if she does,
You have been that Father to me.

Pamela Rasheed

Like a jilted lover who follows his love
And waits at every corner; at every bend
Hoping to be invited in again,
You have not given up on me.
You did not leave me even when I left.

Truly, You are married to the backslider

You did not leave me to my
Own device, but you patiently
kept the watch of my every step,
And gladly entered to rescue me
When I was at my ropes end.

I could not run Father,
I could not hide it all anymore,
It was time; your time
To rescue, deliver and set me free.
You Lord, see me, all of me,
And helped me; Blessed be your Name!

Co-Author's Exhortation
Hide and Seek

*If then you have been raised up with Christ,
keep seeking the things above, where Christ is,
seated at the right hand of God.
For you have died, and your life is hidden
with Christ in God.*

(Colossians 3:1, 3)

WHERE CAN I GO *from Your Spirit?*

WHERE CAN I FLEE *from Your presence?*

PSALM 139:7

Life has a way of presenting many challenges. Some people embrace the unpleasant challenges because they feel that some rain must fall on each life. Others learn to cope with the traumas of life with the reassuring hope that trouble doesn't always last. However, some may feel compelled to resort to substances like drugs, alcohol, gambling, or engaging in activities like sex as a means to escape pain which is not a sustainable solution. These temporary solutions often lead to a vicious cycle where the individual feels a desperate need for another hit or score to alleviate their discomfort.

On the other hand, when one becomes tired of being lost, hurt, and disgusted in life, the only lasting remedy is the Prince of Peace, Christ Jesus. He gives everlasting joy and abiding peace. Only when you begin to draw nearer to your Refuge, Christ Jesus, can your strength, true satisfaction, mercy, and grace be found. In Psalm 105, the Psalmist remembers God's faithfulness.

At the beginning of her backstory, Pamela thought she was going to the Women's Ministry to "check things out" and see if it appealed to her. However, she had her plans for that auspicious day, and God had already orchestrated His divine plans for Pamela. According to Scripture, "the steps of a good man/woman are ordered by the Lord. . . ." (Psalm 37:23). What she did not know was this was a divine appointment.

Like the story of the Prodigal Son, the time may come for us to arise and come to ourselves. The most memorable thing about the story of the Prodigal Son is that not only is the lost son returning home, but while he is still a long way off, his Father caught a glimpse of him. The Bible says that the Father had compassion for him and ran, embraced, and kissed him. The Father told the servants to bring out the best robe, put it on him, and put a ring on his hand and sandals on his feet. They were also told to bring out the fatted calf and kill it. They were to eat and be merry. Through this wonderful parable, Jesus is teaching about the grace of God.

In the profound message of the prodigal son returning home, we also witness the "seeking" Father. Within the context of this beautiful story, we do not see any form of condemnation, but on the contrary, there is a celebration, merriment, rejoicing, and most of all, forgiveness. The point of the story is that God gladly receives repentant sinners.

When one gives their life to God, there are seasons of various kinds. There are times of great joy and celebration. However, there are also times of testing, loss, and the wilderness experience. No matter how we get there, being in the wilderness is a difficult experience. While away from home, the prodigal faced difficulty that reflected being in the wilderness. He was hungry – no food; no one would help or give him anything – he was destitute.

A parallel is observed between the prodigal's story and Sister Pamela's experience.

By the time of her graduation in 2012, her walk with the Lord was almost non-existent. She reminisces on how she was dead spiritually and emotionally. Then it came to a time when she sought just how she could find a niche in Highland Church's women's ministry. She was broken and hiding by selecting a seat near the exit.

However, while she thought she was hiding, God, like the prodigal's Father, came running to her to embrace her. While the Lord was using the speaker to bring Sister Pamela restoration, she continued to hide by putting up a brave face. But God's love penetrates through the façade, and He threw a robe of compassion and understanding upon her. By the time Sister Pamela realized that the love of God was not trying to expose her but love her back to Himself, she could not hide any longer. While she came seeking a place in ministry, she found God was seeking her.

Moreover, while she attempted to hide behind a smokescreen, her real hiding place was Christ Himself, for we are hidden in Christ, in God. And like the prodigal was still a son to his Father, Pamela realized that the great love of her Heavenly Father saw her coming from a far off and changed her plans to align her heart with His once again.

You, dear reader, may have left the presence of God and drifted away. Like Pamela, you may be hiding behind a mask of bravery and smiles, but God always has you on His mind and will come seeking you or watching vigilantly for your return. And when you return and come seeking Him, you will find Him looking for you a far off.

– Reverend Brenda Collier -

CHAPTER 4
Cavelle Francis's story

At the age of twenty-five, I gave birth to my son, never imagining that I would become a single mother. However, as fate would have it, that's what happened. It was a sorrowful period in my life when caring for my newborn became incredibly challenging. I faced a shortage of resources and was plagued by feelings of hopelessness, fear, and uncertainty. Even purchasing basic necessities like milk and diapers was difficult and sometimes seemed insurmountable.

Then, one Sunday, it all crescendoed, and I found myself down to my last bit of formula for my now 4-month-old baby without any help in view (but God). That day, I worried and wondered where I would get milk to feed my son. I lay down with my baby on the bed, holding my baby on my chest, and said to God, "God, please do something; send help." Then I drifted off to sleep. A few hours later, I was awakened by the lady in whose house I was staying. She said that someone was at the door to see me. I was not expecting any visitors.

When I met the person, It turned out that the person was planning to visit me since I had the baby four months prior but never got the chance to do so until that particular day when my baby had no more formula.

At that visit, I was given money to buy milk, diapers, and other things I needed for my baby and me.

God sent help to me through that person, and that help was not limited to milk and diapers alone, but it was extended to getting help with employment and someone to take care of my baby while I go to work. (Men, by your virtue, were commanded to give into my bosom) Selah.

A Psalm of God's Unfailing Love and Provision

- Cavelle Francis -

You kept your watchful eyes on my daily affairs.

In my distress,
The outcry of my heart was loud in your ears.
You, LORD, attended to the scream of my heart
As a father who tends to the needs of his children.
While I was in my slumber
You sent out Devine help.
Men, by your virtue,
were commanded to give into my bosom.
In the earth, no man heard me
But the one who is concerned with what concerns me.
The faithful one who makes sure of my everyday provisions.

LORD, when the reply to my cry was answered.

My mouth was filled with thanksgiving and praise.
Of a truth, you are the lifter of the head of men.
My hope is established in you forever and ever.
Mighty, are you LORD who knows and sees the affairs of men.
Your watchful eyes see my daily affairs, Selah.

Co-Author's exhortation

Motherhood is a rewarding responsibility, and it has been said that the natural state of motherhood is unselfishness. "When you become a mother, you are no longer the center of your own universe; you relinquish that position to your children." (Jessica Lange).

You are now responsible for this new life, and this has proven to be a huge task to manage, and the management is enlarged for the single mom. The reality is that the needs of a child are many, and the finances needed are major. The financial obligations are vast and can include shelter, food, clothing, medical supplies, daycare, and more, which will also require secure employment.

A reliable, dependable support system of family and friends will always lessen the load for a single mother and be a great convenience, but unfortunately, this is not always an option for many. The duties and obligations can often be overwhelming, and you can feel like you're drowning, which can also lead to feelings of fear, uncertainty, and even inadequacy. The wonderful thing is when you decide to cry out to The Lord for help because Proverbs 15:29 tells us that God hears the prayers of the righteous, and Philippians 4 tells us that God will supply our needs. I also love the fact that 1 Corinthians 10:13 reminds us that God is faithful, reliable, trustworthy, and dependable.

How awesome is our God?

The magnificence of God is genuinely displayed in 1 John 3, as we witness His faithfulness when He moves the hearts of individuals to show compassion and aid those in need. We also see God's trustworthiness in Hebrews 13, when He tells all of us never to forget to show hospitality, even to strangers, because we can be entertaining angels unaware, so the Christian must always be in order as it relates to the Word of God because we are to represent Him here on earth.

The relief that anyone in need experiences when they are on the receiving end and the joy they feel to know that God really heard their prayer is such a faith booster for them.

So let's all remember Luke 10 and the story of the good Samaritan and see the difference you can make in the world when you allow The Lord to touch your heart and bless someone. One act of compassion can go a long way. When you have God in your heart for real, it will always show up in you. Selah

Gloria a Dios. [Glory To God]

Chaplain Dr. Cheryl Y. James

CHAPTER 5
Utterances of women in the Bible that are Psalm-like

Psalmist Women of Praise
Sing unto the Lord

*"Sing unto Him, sing psalms unto Him,
talk ye of all His wondrous works."*
(1 Chronicles 16:9)

*"Let us come before His presence with thanksgiving,
and make a joyful noise unto Him with psalms."*
(Psalm 95:2).

Singing unto the Lord is like presenting Him with a philharmonic concert of what is going on in your heart. It is one of the most joyful experiences of the human heart. In many of the recorded psalms in Scripture, we read of personal and sometimes national triumphs in battles, lamentations in grief and failures, adorations in worship, and heartfelt gratitude to the mighty God of Israel.

As one reads the Book of Psalms, observation is made of the recollections of David, Moses, Solomon, and others. All of these expressions are found in Sacred scripture but not in the Book of Psalms, such as the beautiful song commonly known as the "Song of Moses" (Exodus 15:1 - 18 and Deuteronomy 32:1 - 43).

There were community psalms of thanksgiving when the entire community broke forth to glorify the Holy One of Israel, who delivered them from a crisis. It was a full sway of revelry and joyous singing, dancing, and melodies on stringed instruments like the tambourine.

In the same venue, when an individual experienced a personal victory, fulfillment, or an answer to prayer, the overflowing heart would sing praises unto the Lord. One of the most vivid occurrences of this is seen when King David was so brimming with inner joy as the Ark of the Covenant was being brought back into Jerusalem. The Bible says that David danced before the Lord with all his might, wearing a priestly garment. He danced so energetically that his garment fell off. King David saw it fitting to dance in celebration to honor the God who has chosen him and the children of Israel as covenant partners forever.

However, there were individuals mentioned in the Holy Scriptures who expressed their heartfelt praise to the Lord, but they were not included in the Book of Psalms. These individuals can be found within the pages of the Holy Cannon of Scriptures.

Moreover, this group was not male but rather female. Their utterances are Psalm-like and live on throughout the ages for our meditation and reflection on the Power of God. These women of the Bible are Miriam, Deborah, Hannah, and Mary. Each of these individuals demonstrated their devotion and adoration to God because of His faithfulness, love, and sovereignty.

You see, many of the Psalms were born out of crises that ultimately resulted in the praise of victory and triumphed through faith. Being challenged with a lost or forgotten dream, they cried out to the Lord with thanksgiving because God showed Himself mighty in each of their circumstances. Just like King David, when his heart was overwhelmed with joy and gratitude as the Lord's presence (represented by the Ark of the Ark) re-entered Jerusalem, these mighty women of God also experienced an outburst of song, tears, and such words of adoration and faith.

Let us take a moment and examine their songs: "Psalms" of thanksgiving and praise.

1. Miriam: Israel's First Woman of Worship and Praise

The Praise of Victory

Miriam, whose name means "rebellion," was known as the first female prophet in the Scripture. The first time she is mentioned in the scripture, not as Miriam, but as the sister of Moses, is when she sits and watches the basket that held her baby brother, Moses, floating along the river to destiny. This little infant Moses would become the well-respected leader in Israel's tumultuous history, was coddled by the eyes of his sister Miriam before he would grow into manhood and deliver her and the children of Israel out of bondage.

She was later named "Miriam," the prophet in Exodus 15:20-21. It was during this great deliverance that Miriam took her tambourine and led the Israelite women in worship and praise saying:

> *"Sing to the Lord,*
> *For He has triumphed gloriously!*
> *The horse and its rider*
> *He has thrown into the sea!"*
>
> *(Exodus 15:21)*

Observe how Miriam turned the nation of Israel's triumph over Pharaoh and his pursuing army into a psalm of praise. She led the women in singing, dancing, and playing the tambourine after crossing the Red Sea. Her words of jubilant praise are forever etched in the history of Israel as a major part of Israel's deliverance. This is known as the Song of Miriam.

2. Deborah: Israel's Female Judge with a Psalm of Praise

A Song of Victory

Deborah, another dynamic leader in Israel's history, is best known for her wisdom, guidance, and courageous abilities to lead Israel as a judge. She is identified as the only woman judge and is noted on Israel's list of topmost judges. The scriptures do not give any information about her early years. However, there is evidence that she was a homemaker, the wife of Lapidoth (Judges 4:4), and she is known as "a mother in Israel" (Judges 5:7).

Deborah means "bee" in the Hebrew language. It has been stated that this formidable woman of God was like a "bee" during peaceful times and a "wasp" during times of war, which implies that she was exceptionally fierce. There was nothing timid about her because she was confident in her God and her call. The Lord commanded Deborah to send the troops out to destroy Sisera (Judges 4:6, 7). Under her leadership, Barak and the Israelite army were led into battle.

This amazing psalm-like song of praise attributed to Deborah and Barak is a lengthy one reflecting their victory through reminiscing the details of their triumphs. The destruction of the Canaanite power was immortalized in one of the finest examples of Hebrew poetry. It is the entire chapter of Judges chapter 5, consisting of 31 verses. However, we will only highlight the scope of their song as it relates to this book.

> *"That the leaders took the lead in Israel,*
> *that the people offered themselves willingly,*
> *bless the Lord!"*
>
> *"Hear, O kings; give ear, O princes; to the Lord I will sing;*
> *I will make melody to the Lord, the God of Israel".*
>
> *"Lord, when you went out from Seir,*
> *when you marched from the region of Edom,*
> *the earth trembled, and the heavens dropped,*
> *yes, the clouds dropped water".*
>
> *'The mountains quaked before the Lord,*
> *even Sinai before the Lord, the God of Israel".*

In his Introduction to the Old Testament, Robert H. Pfeiffer writes: "The song of Deborah is the finest masterpiece of Hebrew poetry" that "deserves a place among the best songs of victory ever written." The first thing to note is praise is given unto the Lord because the leaders (Deborah and Barak) took the lead in Israel, and under their leadership, the people of Israel offered themselves willingly (vs 2). A call throughout the land to all human kings, princes, and all dignitaries to pay attention to how they will sing and make melody to the God of Israel. Why? Because they verbally declare the Lord's awesome greatness where the heavens dropped, the clouds dropped like water, and the mountains quaked before Him and His astounding and awesome presence.

In Judges Chapter 4, verses 7-9, Deborah writes that the villagers ceased in Israel until she, a mother in Israel, arose. When she used the phrase "the villagers ceased," she was referring to how the Israelites feared going out on the main highways because they feared molestation. Therefore, they traveled the back roads because of the Canaanite oppression.

However, When God raised up Deborah, there was a turnaround of events. He used Deborah to bring new life to Israel and to nurture the conditions that would sustain the children of Israel. Therefore, a renewed call to praise and glorify the God of Israel. Deborah urges them to give thanks and bless the Lord for the victory.

3. Hannah: A Women's Sincere Longing and Fulfillment

A Psalm of Thanksgiving

During the time of the judges, Israel was steeped in idolatry, materialism, and a ruthless way of life. This was a time when there were few Israelites who were devoted to the Lord. The keynote describing them was "every man did what was right in his own eyes" (Judges 21:25). Yet, the book of 1 Samuel opens with the introduction to a woman of faith who had a difficult plight of being barren. Like so many women, Hannah knew the deep agonizing pain of being unable to conceive a child. Her husband, Elkanah, also had another wife who bore him children. The Scriptures reveal that Elkanah loved his wife Hannah and treated her extremely well.

However, during biblical times, the idea of barrenness was believed to have a connotation of God's disapproval. It also fostered the idea that the barren woman is less than a woman - a concept that is still prevalent among women today. The inability to conceive a child is a pain many interpret as a punishment from God because of some past sin or inadequacy. Hannah's story is the biblical account where a woman with an empty womb seeks her God with a heart full of faith. What gives Hannah's story more commiseration is her nemesis, Peninnah, her husband's other wife.

Peninnah was not only fertile, but she antagonized Hannah until the taunting became unbearable. The Bible says, "And her rival used to provoke her grievously to irritate her because the Lord had close her (Hannah) womb." (1 Samuel 1:6). One day, Hannah was so perplexed by Peninnah's pestering that she was not able to eat. Therefore, she went to the temple to pray, where she sought the Lord and pleaded for God to bless her with a son. Her prayer exhibits desperate selflessness because she vowed to give the child back to God for His use in divine service (1 Samuel 1:11). As she fervently beseeched the Lord, her mouth moved, but there was no auditory sound. This resulted in the elderly priest, Eli misconstruing her actions as being one who was drunk, and he rebuked her. But Hannah replied that she was not a drunk but a woman presenting a petition to the Lord. Here are the words of Hannah's Prayer, which is a Psalm:

Blessed In The Detours Of Life

"My heart exalts in the Lord; my horn is exalted in the Lord.

My mouth derides my enemies because I rejoice in your salvation.

"There is none holy like the Lord: for there is none besides you;

there is no rock like our God.

Talk no more so very proudly; let not arrogance come from your mouth;

for the Lord is a God of knowledge, and by him, actions are weighed.

The bows of the mighty are broken, but the feeble bind on strength.

Those who were full have hired themselves out for bread,

but those who were hungry have ceased to hunger.

The barren has borne seven,

but she who has many children is forlorn.

The Lord kills and brings to life; he brings down Sheol and raises up.

The Lord makes poor and makes rich; he brings low, and he exalts.

He raises up the poor from the dust; he lifts the needy from the ash heap

to make them sit with princes and inherit a seat of honor.

For the pillars of the earth are the Lord's

and on them, he has set the world.

"He will guard the feet of his faithful ones,

but the wicked shall be cut off in darkness,

for not by might shall a man prevail.

The adversaries of the Lord shall be broken to pieces;

against them, he will thunder in heaven.

The Lord will judge the ends of the earth;

he will give strength to his king and exalt the horn of his anointed."

(1 Samuel 2:1-10)

Hannah's faith was rewarded, and because the Lord heard her prayer, she named her son Samuel, which means _heard by God_. Hannah obeyed the Mosaic Law when she honored her vow to the Lord. It was probably very difficult for her to take little Samuel to the temple and leave him there. According to the Hebrew custom, She most certainly nursed him for several years, giving her time to convey to Samuel her own sense of deep reverence and piety and to bond her heart with her firstborn. Yet, her obedience resulted in a great blessing because God blessed her with other offspring (1 Samuel 2:20-21).

Hannah expresses her gratitude to God for His unwavering faithfulness. She rejoices in the Lord, acknowledging that no one is comparable to Him. She proclaims His holiness and acknowledges that God is steadfast like a rock.

She also addresses those who are proud and arrogant; and how the Lord weighs their actions (verses 3-5). I believe she was thinking of Peninnah, which is common in psalmist writing. How often do we read about David addressing his triumph over his enemies. Similarly, Hannah addresses her personal triumphs and glorifies God for His answer to prayer because He had provided salvation for His people.

Hannah makes mention of God's holiness (v. 2), power (v. 2), wisdom (v. 3), justice (v. 3), sovereignty, and providence (vv. 6 - 10) in her prayer. The whole point of Hannah's inspired psalm of thanksgiving and praise is that people should trust in the Lord.

4. Mary: A Woman of Purity in Praise

A Psalm from the Woman Blessed Above All Women

Mary, the mother of Jesus, is distinguished among women and called "blessed and highly favored." Her name, Mary, translates as bitter, rebelliousness, and beloved. However, she was nothing like that, for she was neither bitter nor rebellious; but she is greatly loved throughout the ages. She is commonly referred to as the Virgin Mary, which sometimes implies that she remained a virgin throughout her lifetime. But that is not true because the Bible makes it clear that she was the mother of the other siblings of Jesus, James, Joses (a form of Joseph), Simon and Jude, and unnamed sisters mentioned in the Gospels of Matthew (13:56) and Mark (6:3). There was no other human being closer to Jesus on earth than His mother, Mary. '

As a young virgin maiden, God hand-picked Mary to conceive, give birth, raise, and nurture our Lord Jesus Christ. In her own astounding words of adoration and praise to God, Mary acknowledges her unique role in history - a role that was incredibly distinctive, to the point where it was difficult to comprehend.

I once met a Jewish lady, a medical doctor by profession. She told me that she was intrigued by the life of Jesus. She said it was so evident that if there was ever going to be a Promised One coming, it was Jesus, Israel's long-awaited Messiah. I found this inspiring, yet she hesitated when I inquired about her placing her faith in Him. But what she said next really shocked me. She said: "I am a doctor, a woman of science. And one thing I know for sure, there is no way a woman can become pregnant and still be a virgin. The virgin birth is one of the main pillars of the Christian faith. And it is Mary who validates the fact that she was a virgin. After being told that she was going to be the mother of the Messiah, she asked the angel, "How can these things happen, since I have not ever known a man?" (Luke 1:34). Her virginity is the key here, because of two distinct factors; God prophetically said that it would be a sign that a virgin would conceive (Isaiah 7:14); and the child conceived would be as a result of the overshadowing of the Holy Spirit. The conceived child is referred to in Matthew's Gospel as a holy thing.

Mary's psalm of praise is universally known as Mary's Magnificat (Luke 1:46 - 55)

And Mary said,

"My soul magnifies the Lord,

and my spirit rejoices in God, my Savior,

for he has looked on the humble estate of his servant.

For behold, from now on, all generations will call me blessed;

for he who is mighty has done great things for me,

and holy is his name.

And his mercy is for those who fear him
from generation to generation.
He has shown strength with his arm;
he has scattered the proud in the thoughts of their hearts;
he has brought down the mighty from their thrones
and exalted those of humble estate;
he has filled the hungry with good things,
and the rich he has sent away empty.

He has helped his servant Israel,
in remembrance of his mercy,
as he spoke to our fathers,
to Abraham and his offspring forever."

Mary's Psalm of Praise glorifies God using the term 'magnify.' This powerful word means to deem or declare great, make great, or extol. In other words, in Mary's Psalm of Praise, she places the highest praise on God to celebrate Him. In so doing, Mary esteems God highly for looking down on her in her low estate, and He lifts her to a place where all humanity, every generation, will speak blessings upon her. In v. 49, She claims that the Almighty has done great things for her.

These great things speak of God doing magnificent, excellent, splendid, and wonderful things for her. She applauds God's acts toward her and then blesses Him by declaring holy in His name.

The beauty of Mary's Magnificat has been put to music throughout the history of the Christian church.

Reverend Brenda Collier

CHAPTER 6

Backstory
~ Chaplain Dr. Cheryl Y. James

Several years ago, back when my children were very young, I had the incredible opportunity to attend a women's conference in Atlanta, Georgia. My husband was wonderfully supportive, taking care of the kids and even requesting time off from work to do so. I was fortunate to have my mother join me on the trip, and together we enjoyed a spiritually charged weekend at a stunning resort.

After the retreat ended, my mother and I headed back to the airport with a sense of enthusiasm, reflecting on the amazing time we had. We checked in our luggage with TWA Airlines, the carrier operating then. However, when we arrived at the boarding gate to check in with the attendants, we were informed that our seats were considered standby, and there was a possibility that we might not be able to board this flight due to the limited availability of seats. Although we were previously assigned seats on the plane, it now appeared they were placing others before us. In addition, the airline would not even confirm that they would be able to guarantee us a seat on another flight for the entire day. The staff did not appear friendly nor express any compassion for our situation. I told them we had already checked our luggage, but they seemed unconcerned and said it could be placed in a locker at Kennedy Airport until we picked it up. They told us to have a seat and would speak to us after they were through with the boarding of the plane.

Mom and I looked at one another with unbelief as we sat quietly. I was filled with anguish, anxiety, a little anger, and a lot of sadness. My thoughts were fixed on the fact that my husband had to return to work the next day, and my delay could inconvenience him and delay him from returning to his job as scheduled. Being worried was an understatement. We had just experienced the most glorious time in the Lord, loving and worshipping our Lord and Savior, Jesus Christ. How could this be happening to us after such a powerfully charged weekend? Mom and I looked at each other with worry in our eyes but made a strong decision to begin to pray and talk to The Lord because it was clear he was the only one with an answer or intervention regarding this situation. The Lord was our only option. We both lowered our heads to pray. I could hear people getting up all around us to get in line for boarding. I glimpsed up and saw the last person enter the door to the airplane ramp, and then the doors were closed.

I refused to accept what my eyes were witnessing because I believed my God had the final say, especially after the miraculous worship experience we just had and that he had made possible for us. In my spirit, I decided to speak God's Word back to Him in prayer and speak the promises He said were mine according to His will. I stood my ground as a child of God and stood on my Faith as I conversed with My heavenly Father. I blocked out everyone, everything, and every voice around me.

I prayed a prayer to God, unlike any prayer I had ever prayed in my entire life. It was clear to me that only the power of God could reverse this situation, which clearly seemed permanent. I had nothing to lose but much to gain because I needed to get home immediately. This was personal to me and for me. I reminded God of how He blessed me with the opportunity to travel, not that he didn't already know this. I told Him about my sincere love for Him, my reverence for Him, and the worship and praise I had just showered on Him throughout the retreat. I reminded Him that I was His child and spoke His promise for His children in the scripture. I kept repeating:

John 15:7-14 to God. I abide in you, Lord and your Word abides in me Father, so I am asking because You said that I could.

James 4. You said Father, I speak your words back to you Lord.

Hebrews 11:6 *I am standing in faith Father. I am seeking you, Lord and you are a rewarder to those who diligently seek You. You said Father. You said Father. I am a child of God.*

John 1:12. Romans 8:28 I need this situation to work out for my good Lord, like your word says.

Matthew 22:37. I love you Lord with all of my heart and soul, and mind.

I need your help Lord, like it says in Isaiah 41: 10, I need your help and your word says that you will help me.

I kept quoting scripture over and over. I kept saying; I stand on your word, Lord. I declare your word Lord. I am standing on faith, Lord. Then as my head remained bowed, I said something so bold that I almost couldn't believe I was saying it. I said, Lord, if this airplane does not make it back to New York safely, I'm okay with not having a seat. Then I said, "But Lord if it will arrive safely, I would like two seats on this airplane for my mom and me."

Then I said, Lord, if everyone on this airplane loves you as I do, then I'm okay with not having a seat. Then I said but Lord, if everyone on the plane is not a believer and a child of God who loves you like I do, will you please give mom and me your children a seat to go home tonight on this plane. You choose, Lord. Father, if it's your will, it's your choice to select who to remove. Your word says in John 15 that if I abide in you and your Word in me, Lord, I am allowed to ask a desire.

My desire and need, Lord is for Mom and me to go home today.

I began to thank the lord in advance for hearing me and answering my prayer request. Once again, I had nothing to lose but much to gain. I didn't open my eyes but continued to thank God for hearing my prayer and answering my prayer request. I heard the TWA agent speak over the microphone that flight number 333 was preparing for takeoff. I never looked up but continued to repeat words of love and thanks in advance to my Lord. I didn't let up.

Miraculously the boarding door swung open, and two people came out and walked over to the desk where the agents were seated. The TWA Agent then called our name and told us to come forward. We were rushed down the ramp by a gentleman who told us to run because the plane was in takeoff mode, and we needed to hurry. When I looked back to say thank you, he was gone. I don't know where he came from, nor do I understand how fast he disappeared. When we stepped on the plane, one of the flight attendants seemed a little irritated, possibly at the delay, and said to another attendant, "Where are they going to sit?" The response was, one here and the other over there.

We both were placed in two first-class seats. They were not together but on opposite sides of the aisle and not close together, so I only assumed that the two people who exited the plane were not flying together.

I had a window seat in first class. I was overwhelmed not just because the miracle and answered prayer had just happened but also because My Father, My Lord, and My King had just given me and my mother a first-class seat. I had never had the pleasure nor the finances to ride in first class in my life. As the tears flowed down my face, I tried to reason how God just blew my mind. Was this really happening? Did God actually do this for me? The love he just showed me is beyond my wildest dreams. I couldn't speak as my throat quivered. I said nothing to the man to who I was seated next. I couldn't stop crying as I gazed out the window into heaven, grateful to The Lord for what he had just done for me. I was overwhelmed with thanksgiving and praise.

The Lord removed two people from the plane for me; no Way, I thought.

When we returned to New York, I told my mom what I prayed to God. She looked at me and shook her head, saying, "Cheryl, you can't talk to God like that." I laughed and said Mom, God knew my heart and how I love and reverence Him over everything and everyone. Our situation was major, and only the grace of God could have helped us. He honored His word Mom, and faith moved His hand. My Faith in speaking His Word back to Him touched Him because He is faithful, and scripture says He will not allow His Word to return to Him unfulfilled. His

Word is sharper than any double-edged sword, and His Word performed the work for us both. I then said he honored my request, Mom, so it must have been His will to do so.

A Psalm Of Remembrance and Consolation

- Chaplain Dr. Cheryl Y. James -

How Excellent is Your name in all the earth.
How majestic is Your Holy name
You are worthy of all praise - Selah.

My Father, My Lord,
my heart is overwhelmed with gratitude
when I think of how you rescued my situation.
In my earsplitting unrest,
my distress, and piercing thoughts,
you reminded me of Your Sacred Texts,
Your Holy Writings, and your Testaments.

You calmed me and wiped away my agitation.
You brought my heart and mind over to your peace
and tranquility,
burning away all my agitation.

Blessed In The Detours Of Life

My God, My God,
oh, how You melted my tense thoughts.
I so remember, My Father, how You freed my anxious mind.
You removed the chains that wrapped my mind
and the arrows that pierced my heart.
You saw those who were unmoved by my pained face.
Yes, Lord, you quieted my spirit so I could breathe
and compose myself.
You breathe, Lord, poured into my bronchi and
I gingerly remembered who I was.

I recall, recollect, and reminisce of
Your profound love for me and how you
straightway grasped hold and claimed me as your own.
You said I was your peculiar treasure.
Oh, how you lifted my thoughts and pondering as
I inhaled your promises and faith into my remembrance.
I remember I remember, yes, I remember,
and I piped up with Your Sword.
Your two-edged sword, I spoke back to you,
and it annihilated the enemy's plan to disrupt my family schedule.
I sputtered your power into the atmosphere.

Chaplain Dr. Cheryl Y. James

I declared your voice back to the Heaven
and you collected and received them.
My God, My God, you canceled the enemy's assignment.
You revoked, retracted, and reversed it.
You were my lawyer, My defender, My Savior, and; My Lord.
You suddenly and immediately positioned me in your sky.
I was able to see Your heavens as
I traveled through Your atmosphere.
How excellent was the view of your beautiful white clouds.

My Lord and My King,
you gave me a seat at your table.
A table I was unfamiliar with.
The best seat in your court Lord.
A first-class seat with fine China instead of paper plates.
As you guided me home safely by
Your force of celestial beings, I was overtaken with emotion.
The water rolled down my face, and you collected it.
You proved Yourself Mighty and Strong.
You let the atmosphere know who you were.
You were and are, and will always be

The Alpha and Omega.
You are, I Am.

You are the omnipotent,
omniscient, and the omnipresent God of this universe.
I overcame because you overcame the world.
How excellent is your name in all the earth. Selah

Author's Exhortation

Desperate situations call for desperate measures, but often many people give up because they run out of fuel and lose the strength to persevere. Minister Chery's situation was desperate, but she prayed a desperate prayer and waited on God with expectation. God did not need a reminder of what He has done for her in the past, but He certainly took delight in the fact that Minister James reminded him because she remembers God's goodness and thanked him for it.

When you have won little battles and graduated to new and higher levels in your faith, greater battles and more desperate circumstances will come your way; count it a pleasure that God deems you fit to take on yet another one.

It is vital to remember those smaller battles that you have overcome and don't forget to give God Praise each time. I charged my students to _"remember not to forget, and do not forget to remember"_ what God has done, and as you do, give Him Praise.

You see, God's ego is fed by our worship and praise. It is no secret that true worship and praise move the hand of God. He loves it when we just glorify Him in everything, great or small. In-Kind David's desperate moment, he said: *But thou art holy, O thou that inhabits the praises of Israel (Psalm 22:3 KJV).*

God dwells in our praises; in His presence, nothing stays the same; miracles happen; chains are broken, situations change, and lives are transformed.

When David stood before the giant, Goliath, he already saw the victory because he knew the God who helped in times past when he slayed the lion, and the bear was the same God who had his back at that moment.

David said to the Philistine,
"You come against me with sword and spear and javelin,
but I come against you in the name of the LORD Almighty,
the God of the armies of Israel, whom you have defied.

1 Samuel 17:45 (NIV)

So, my dear friends, even when some battles seem insignificant, give God praise for the victories, knowing that overcoming those small difficulties builds up your spiritual stamina for greater battles that bring greater victories to keep you scaling upwards to greater heights with God.

I encourage you to read 1 Samuel 17 and Psalm 22.

Pamela Rasheed

CHAPTER 7

Geraldine Simmons

I wrote this psalm in reference to one of the many things God has done for me. Most recently, He showed me that I was protected from harm's way.

I had to go to the Internal Revenues Office after learning that my social security number had been used in identity theft. I was in a state of confusion. However, I decided to visit a store on Queens Blvd. Upon removing my shopping cart containing all my personal belongings, I realized that one of my bracelets was missing. I retraced my steps back to the car and searched inside but to no avail. Subsequently, I revisited the area I had been to earlier, hoping that I might have dropped it there, but my search was in vain. As a last resort, I returned to the spot where I had initially parked, only to find that someone else had occupied it. Despite feeling bewildered, I proceeded to search for another parking spot. Unfortunately, I failed to notice that I had left my shopping cart unattended in that lot. Eventually, I managed to find another parking spot, but for some inexplicable reason, I experienced difficulty while attempting to park my vehicle.

So, I decided to leave and go to College Point to another shopping area. After arriving there, I couldn't decide which store to go into. Finally, I decided to go into Shop Rite (the supermarket). That is when I realized I didn't have my shopping cart. Now, I am truly in a panic. All I could think of was how foolish I was. How could I have done that? My credit cards, license, phone, and all my identification, even a letter from the IRS, were in my bag in that shopping cart. Bewildered, I thought, "Oh my goodness, I just gave someone all my information."

Suddenly, a voice inside my mind urged me to return to the previous parking lot. My thoughts were, "How could it still be there? What is the sense?" More than an hour had passed since I had left the cart unattended on Queens Blvd. Given the amount of time that had elapsed, it was likely that by the time I returned, more than 90 minutes would have gone by. The voice within my spirit wouldn't stop prodding me to go back. As I continued to hear, "Go back, go back," I said to myself, "What the heck, what did I have to lose."

On my way back, I couldn't believe how calm I was. I needed to see for myself that the cart wasn't there. When I reached Queens Blvd, I parked the car and started walking back to where I believed I had left the cart. And to my surprise, it was there. If you are familiar with Queens Blvd, you know there is always heavy traffic there. People were going up and down, passing the cart. I truly believe God dispatched angels to protect it, or it was made invisible to the eye. By the way, on my way back home after retrieving the shopping cart, something extraordinary occurred. I heard the same voice, directing my attention to the fact that my lost bracelet was actually located inside my car, between the seat and the console. Without hesitation, I looked down, and behold, there it was! It's good to know that God's right by my side.

A Psalm of God's Protection
Geraldine Simmons

Father God, I thank you!
for always being near
Even when I didn't know it
you were there.
Always covering and protecting
me from harm's way
You have done so many things
in my life to show how much you care.

How a father protects his child
through sickness, pain,
sorrow and confusion,
You are always there

You have brought me through
many trials and tribulations
I had to bear it, and I am so
thankful for your blessings,
Without you, I would be in total despair

So, forever I will thank you
in the name of your son Jesus Christ,
because you for letting me know that you are there.

Author's Exhortation

Unexpected and unpleasant circumstances have the potential to cause stress that can be overwhelming, leading to confusion and disorientation. We rattle our brains to find a solution that clouds our train of thoughts even more. At times, it may seem like a prayer won't bring a solution because, more often than not, we have boxed God in and think we are the ones to solve every situation. But knowing who to call on in these moments is where our victory lies in all battles, great or small. Solutions and victories are won when we call on our creator and savior.

Kind David faced a great and unpleasant situation at Ziklag. It may have been pointless to ask God for direction because his human "fix-it-now" attitude could have dictated his own solution, but he recognized that he needed God's direction.

This situation is recorded in 1 Samuel chapter 30, where David asked God for direction.

> *"And David enquired at the LORD, saying,*
> *Shall I pursue after this troop?*
> *Shall I overtake them?*
> *And He answered him, Pursue:*
> *for thou shalt surely overtake them,*
> *and without fail recover all" (1 Samuel 30:8).*

As sister Geraldine faced the situation, she asked God's direction, and He replied. I encourage you not to think God does not hear or see you in your circumstances. His words said that his ears are not too heavy that they cannot hear, nor his hands too short that they cannot reach us when we call on him in pureness of heart. Salvation is instantaneous, but sanctification is a process. Daily, we need to renew ourselves before the Lord and seek his cleansing and directions every day. Do not let unconfessed sins keep you away from his loving care.

Behold, the LORD'S hand is not shortened,
that it cannot save; neither his ear heavy, that it cannot hear:
But your iniquities have separated between you and your God,
and your sins have hid his face from you, that he will not hear.

(Isaiah 59:1-2)

Call on Him from a pure heart in all your circumstances, and listen for His voice of guidance, direction, and peace.

Pamela Rasheed

CHAPTER 8

A Psalm of Remembrance of God's Provision

Lavonne Jackson-Wright

I recall a time when my van required repairs to pass the State inspection. I prayed and asked the Lord which mechanic to take the van to. He answered and directed me where to take it. However, when the mechanic checked it out, he said a few different things were wrong with it. I told him to go ahead and fix it.

The price to get the job done to pass inspection was very high, and I did not have the cash to pay at that time. So, I put the matter before the Lord and believed that God would work it out − He would provide.

Then out of nowhere, I got a call from one of my credit card companies who said they were increasing my credit line. The money I needed to fix the van was the amount, and more on my credit card increased. I was able to pay the mechanic on my credit card.

Now it was time for me to take the van for inspection, but when the mechanic took it, it failed. I was advised that the van needs to be driven for a while and then brought back for a re-check to see if it is ready to pass inspection.

Whenever I brought it back to be inspected, the technician said, "No, it's not ready." You must drive it again. I did this three times. During these times of setbacks and delays, God made ways for me to get to work, church, etc. I remember one Monday, my schedule was so busy, and I needed to get around to different places, and the Lord made way for me by sending Ubers on that day to get to work, home, to the doctor's office, and the mechanic, and every time it was paid for.

God is so faithful. He has promised that He will not give us more than we can bear, and He raises people up to help us when we need help. Without them even knowing what you're going through. That is His hands in the situations and circumstances of our lives. God is so faithful. The van eventually passed inspection, and I am driving it now. I am grateful to God for this.

A Psalm of Praise to God for He is my Strength – Lavonne

I will praise you, oh Lord!
For you have been the strength of my life.
When I don't know what to do
You give me peace of mind.
You take me away with you.
To rest in your peaceful presence.
To take times of quietness and
meditation with you.

To hear what you are
saying I should do next.
You directed my steps and
You give songs of praise and worship!
As I keep my focus on you and
not the problem or the issues.

You take me into that place.
Of worship, praise, and prayer
You take me to Your word
To Bible reading to hear your voice.

In those times, I hear your

Blessed In The Detours Of Life

still small voice inside speaking to me.
I wait patiently, heavenly father
For you to give me the answers
I need to hear.
And as I lay all of my petitions before you.
It is you who is in control of my life
and the direction I must take.

Oh, how I love you, Lord!
You've been my closest and best friend.
You've always been by my side
and I appreciate you for this.

I'm never alone!
Even though you may not be a physical person.
You are definitely there in the spirit.
I can most certainly feel and sense
the comfort of your Holy Spirit within me.

God, you have been my everything.
You have been so faithful!
In every trial that comes my way.
When I am faced with big decisions
In my life, to make
I want to run and hide.
But you said no, don't hide but

Come to me, and I will lead and guide you.
And You let me know what I should do next.

You, Oh God, have made me
stronger, wiser, more alert,
and aware of what's happening
in my life and around me. And
You have drawn me closer to you.

God, I'm so grateful that you never leave me.
You have seen me through it all.
You have stood up within me and besides me.
Heavenly Father, you have made
ways out of no way for me.
I am so grateful for you, Lord.

Thank you for those quiet times with you.
You are my unique, loving, kind,
and powerful God.
I love you, Lord
Thank you for you.

Co-Author's Exhortation

We are asked not to trust in horses or chariots but in the name of the Lord, our strong tower, and we can run into Him and be safe. As we put our hope in God's almighty and powerful hands, He has a way of bringing us through the storms and difficulties of life. We are His children and the sheep of His pasture, and unable to care for the details of life without the great Shepherd of our souls. He promises to lead us beside the still waters, restore our souls, and lead us into the right path for His name's sake.

It's encouraging to be able to lift our eyes unto the hills by faith, from where all our help comes from in life. God is our Jehovah Jireh, the Lord who will provide. He sees the future as well as the past and present. He can anticipate and provide for what we need. When we pray to Jehovah Jireh, we are praying to a God who sees the situation beforehand, and He can work it out.

In the book of (Gen. 22:1-2, AMPC) we read, "After these events, God tested and proved Abraham and said to him, Abraham! And he said, Here I am. [God] said, take now your son, your only son Isaac, whom you love, and go to the region of Moriah; and offer him there as a burnt offering upon one of the mountains of which I will tell you." Now Isaac was Abraham's favorite son of his old age, and the last thing he wanted to do was sacrifice his son and take his life away.

We do know, however, that Abraham was a man of faith who trusted God; they had a great relationship. As a result, Abraham was called a friend of God. So, he obeyed God's command; he built an altar of wood, bound his only son on it, reached out his hand, and took a knife to slay him. Then we read that something amazing had happened. (Gen. 22:11-12, AMPC) "But the Angel of the Lord called to him from heaven and said, Abraham, Abraham! He answered, Here I am. And He said, do not lay your hand on the lad or do anything to him; for now, I know that you fear and revere God, since you have not held back from Me or begrudged giving Me your son, your only son."

We witness how Abraham's faith in God and His word resulted in Isaac's rescue. As a result, we learn how God's name came into being. We read in, (Gen. 22:13-14, AMPC) "Then Abraham looked up and glanced around, and behold, behind him was a ram caught in a thicket by his horns. And Abraham went and took the ram and offered it up for a burnt offering and an ascending sacrifice instead of his son! So, Abraham called the name of that place The Lord Will Provide. And it is said to this day, On the mount of the Lord it will be provided."

Along our life's journey, we must recognize and thank Jehovah Jireh for all His many blessings, including, yet not limited to, the provision in a time of need.

Sister Lavonne's story reminds us that the God we swerve is not only the God of those mentioned in the Bible, but He is our God in the present. We realize His blessings never end because He is a God of infinite grace and love yesterday, today, and forever more. We praise and worship Him for who He is, His loving provision, His presence, His protection, and everything needed to sustain us is His demonstration of Love and Faithfulness.

Evangelist Ida Mack-Humphrey

CHAPTER 9

Joyann's Backstory

It all started with lower back pains, nothing more. One evening as I lay on the floor, I dosed off. Suddenly I woke up to find the most beautiful angel floating directly over me. I thought I was dreaming, so I closed my eyes; when I reopened them, she was still there. She was clothed in all white with gorgeous long golden hair, wings, and a scepter in her hand emulating a bright light around her, and then she disappeared.

A few days later, I felt some discomfort on the right side of my stomach. The next thing I knew, I was doing tests and scans, and according to the doctor, it did not look good, they were talking about the "c" word. The fear stepped in, and even though the blood work was good, nothing could be determined until surgery, for the cyst was the size of a basketball. A two-hour surgery turned into six hours, as the cyst ruptured and was very challenging. I had six months of chemo even though it could not be graded. During that year, I had several procedures, some very painful. Needless to say, it was traumatic and scary. So, from being a completely healthy person, I've now been seeing doctors on a weekly basis for almost a year. The healing was difficult, I could barely eat, and nothing stayed in my stomach. I remember one night I said to the Lord, "If I must die, let me go back to Trinidad (my home) and die." Then

I heard his voice, so peacefully; "EAT, WHETHER IT COMES OUT THROUGH THE FRONT OR BACK, EAT." I then eat a slice of toast, which I can consume.

Being born into a Presbyterian home, I knew of God, went to church, and prayed. However, I knew very little about the Holy Spirit. I had started going to a "non-denominational "church around that time, where they thought about the Holy Spirit, healing, and the Word. I learned to listen and hear his voice. My Rhema scripture came, and in Mark 11, verses: 22-24, "Whatever you say with your mouth and believe with your heart, you will receive what you ask for." This scripture increased my faith in believing in Jesus's healing. After all, HE said it; "by my stripes, you are healed." This was my path to recovery and healing, combined with prayers from my family, friends, and church. Prayer is powerful, and it is our direct connection to God Almighty.

I did not receive a miracle; in fact, words cannot describe the pain, both physically and mentally. I have asked, "Why me?" I know I will never get the answer.

It is now ten years, and I am completely healed, healthy, and whole. I refuse to accept the diagnosis, not that I am in denial, but I take God at his living and written Word. HE is God almighty all by Himself. I hope my Psalm of gratitude will encourage someone who needs it to trust Abba, regardless of the outcome. It is not an easy thing to do when you are in pain and everything looks so bleak, but never give up on GOD, for HE cannot lie. I make it personal with God; he is "my father," and I choose to trust him always. I had grown in faith at that time, so I believed his word that "I am healed." The physical scar is still visible to this day, but I have fully recovered. My gratitude to our Lord Jesus is beyond words.

A Psalm of Gratitude for Healing

- Joyann Jagdeo -

I will praise you in the morning,
I will sing a new song,
I will dream of you and your goodness.
For the Lord promised us good things,
He created us; He is our Father. Selah.

Oh my Lord, My Savior, I cannot rest.
My strength is drained from my body,
and my bones are weak.
Yet you promised to protect me and keep me safe.

When the fire came,
He shielded me and walked through the furnace with me.
Though burnt, I was not scarred,
Because my Abba father quenched the flames
and dried every tear from my eyes.
Thank you, my Lord.

He knew my pain and sent his angels to comfort me.

Joyann Jagdeo

I waited for a miracle, but it did not come.
I cried unto the Lord with a weak voice
and did not hear him. Oh Lord,
where are you, did you abandon me?

He is always with me;
like a warm summer breeze, I feel your presence.
You are so gracious.
A sweet floral scent came over me
and I was renewed.
I know your works and your ways,
they are so perfect and flawless. Selah

I believe.
My heart overflows with gratitude
for your light and beauty surrounds me.
When I doubt,
I remember your love without limits or boundaries.
Just as the waters flow in the ocean,
and the stars light up the skies,
so is your love, my Abba Father.

The Lord is my healer,
I will call upon him forever.

As I stretched out my hands, he lifted me up,
like a Father with his child.
My mouth will speak thanksgiving and praises of you,
My precious Lord, my God, my savior
My trust is in you forever and ever.

Author's exhortation

Psalms 41 in the Bible contains one of the most comforting Psalms for those who suffer from illnesses. The Psalmist, King David, faced many adversities in his life before and during his reign as Israel's second King. But while he also won countless victories, he faced betrayals by those close to him, including his own son Absolom and his trusted friend, Ahithophel. As a shepherd and later as king, David constantly put his trust in God and confessed and repented his sins. He had an awful illness at the time, so it was not unusual for him to confess any wrongdoing and turn to God in faith and hope for recovery.

When David wrote this Psalm of lament, he was not only seriously ill, but his enemies hoped he would die. Just imagine the loneliness amidst being afraid. But he knew who his God was. His affirmation in this situation was, *"The Lord will sustain him on his sickbed and restore him from his bed of illness." (v 3).*

In times when we as believers face serious or life-threatening illness, betrayals, and feelings of physical helplessness, it is a time when our faith in God is tested. Uncertainty floods our minds and brings the fear of death. Fear causes the sick to question the strength of their faith in God, and even the most devout may ask, "Do I even have the faith of a mustard seed to believe in divine healing?" It can be natural and easier for humans to trust doctors and their prescribed remedies than trust God because we do not see God. I do encourage you to trust God wholly. Repent of unconfessed sin and ask for healing, as well as faith to trust God for your healing. Isaiah 53:5 says, *"But he was wounded for our transgressions, he was bruised for our iniquities: the chastisement of our peace was upon him, and with his stripes, we are healed."*

David affirms in Psalms 23:4, *"Yea, though I walk through the valley of the shadow of death, I will fear no evil: for thou art with me; thy rod and thy staff they comfort me."*

So, dear readers, I encourage you to repent of your wrongdoing in the eyes of the Lord, ask for forgiveness from him and anyone you may have hurt, and take God at his work for the healing of your body, mind, and spirit. He is able!

Pamela Rasheed

CHAPTER 10

Who is God to Us?

Chaplain, Dr. Cheryl Y. James

From the Old Testament to The New Testament, it is abundantly clear that our God has always been a source of strength, a shoulder to lean on, an ear to listen to our every word - spoken or unsaid, happy or sad, and a voice to provide encouragement and directives.

He has served as our protector, deliverer, and source of provision and strength.

So, please feel free to read these scriptures, which will also offer encouragement and reminds you of who God is. These verses are taken from the King James Version (KJV). God is:

Our way of escape ~ 1 Corinthians 10:13 ~ *There hath no temptation taken you, but such as is common to man: but God is faithful, who will not suffer you to be tempted above that ye are able; but will with the temptation also make a way to escape, that ye may be able to bear it.*

Our Truth ~ John 14:6 ~ *Jesus saith unto him, I am the way, the truth, and the life: no man cometh unto the Father but by me.*

Love ~ 1 John 4:8 ~ *He that loveth not knoweth not God; for God is love*

Longsuffering and Patient ~ 2 Peter 3:9 ~ *The Lord is not slack concerning His promise, as some men count slackness; but is longsuffering toward us, not willing that any should perish, but that all should come to repentance.*

The Way ~ John 14:6 ~ *Jesus saith unto him, I am the way, the truth, and the life: no man cometh unto the Father, but by me.*

Our Help ~ Isaiah 41:13 ~ *For I The Lord thy God will hold thy right hand, saying unto thee, Fear not; I will help you.*

Our Creator ~ Genesis 1:1 ~ *In the beginning, God created the heaven and the earth,*

Our Salvation and Refuge ~ Psalm 62:7 ~ *In God is my salvation and my glory: the rock of my strength, and my refuge is in God.*

Our "I AM" ~ Exodus 3:14 ~ *And God said unto Moses, I Am That I Am: and He said, Thus shalt thou say unto the children of Israel, I Am hath sent me unto you.* 'I am" is present-tense, and it speaks of 'NOW." He is in the <u>now</u> of your situation; not was or will be, but "I am."

Makes The Impossible Possible ~ Luke 18:27 ~ *And He said, The things which are impossible with men are possible with God.*

Merciful ~ Psalm 116:5 ~ *Gracious is the Lord, and righteous; yea, our God is merciful.*

The Light ~ John 8:12 ~ *Then spake Jesus again unto them, saying, I am the light of the world: he that followeth me shall not walk in darkness, but shall have the light of life.*

Compassionate ~ Psalm 86:15 ~ *But thou, O Lord, art a God full of compassion, and gracious, long-suffering, and plenteous in mercy and truth.*

Our Savior ~ John 3: 17 ~ *For God sent not His Son into the world to condemn the world; but that the world through Him might be saved.*

Our Strength and Power ~ 2 Samuel 22:33 ~ *God is my strength and power: and he maketh my way perfect*

Our All-in-All ~ Ephesians 4:6 ~ *One God and Father of all, who is above all, and through all, and in you all.*

The Alpha and Omega, Beginning and Ending ~ Revelation ~ 22:13 ~ *I am Alpha and Omega, the beginning, and the end, the first and the last.*

These Scriptures are just a sample because God is so much more. I trust that as you continue to read the wonderful chapters and personal testimonies in this book of the goodness of God, be encouraged and inspired to also set aside time to meditate on who The Lord is to you and how He rescued you, and He will continue to rescue you in your time of need if you let Him. Read His word, the Holy Bible, daily and be reassured that The Lord loves you beyond measure and He is Faithful to the end.

Blessings To You

Dr. Chaplain Cheryl Y. James

CHAPTER 11

Karen Perez's backstory

My psalm is about my struggles to conceive children. I have been married for 16 years, and this is an obstacle that my husband and I have faced during our marriage. I have done in-vitro fertilization (IVF) countless times to no avail. Thousands of dollars have been spent, and a lot of emotions have been invested. It is heartbreaking and very frustrating. It makes me wonder if I'm being punished. My psalm is a cry out to the lord because I feel like he has forgotten me.

A Psalm of Waiting on God for Child

- Karen Perez's -

Oh Lord, where are you?
I sing praise to your name.
I can feel your presence,
but I haven't heard an answer from you.

I have many, many questions, Lord.
I need you right now.
I need you, Lord.
I need a supernatural miracle.
Only you can do it.

You are great and mighty.
You sit high and look low.
You are a miracle worker.
There is none like you.

Oh Lord, I'm waiting.
Fill me up, Lord; Fill the void.
Cover me, Lord.

Karen Perez

Make the impossible possible.
You have done so much
I am forever grateful,
but did you forget me this time?

Please don't forget about me.
Don't dim my light.
Show me, Lead me.
I believe and trust you, Lord.
I will learn to be content with your will,
for your will is the only way.

Author's Exhortation

God is omniscient, He alone is God and will never leave His throne. He may place a baby in your arms in an unexpected way. Trust Him and never relent.

Naturally, as women, it is expected that our bodies will easily and always want to do what they are ultimately meant to do; to fulfill their God-given function of producing offspring. Individuals who long to become mothers but encounter obstacles may feel a sense of betrayal from their own bodies and, as believers, may also feel let down by God. Many women suffer in silence and feel detached from society because of the taboo of infertility imposed upon couples with the feeling of inadequacy. They cannot help but blame themselves or their spouses and sometimes their past failures or sin.

As a fertility nurse, I have heard the desperate words of women in deep emotional, psychological, and spiritual distress of not being able to conceive or carry a pregnancy to term. There is not much to be said for a woman who has tried relentlessly to have a child, including putting their faith in their doctors and spending all their life savings, even going into debt to try medical technology to no avail.

It is futile to just say to a believer, "Continue to trust God" When they have invested all their faith, only to feel the claws of inadequacy ripping away the very fabric of their existence and trusting God alone with their finite minds does not bring a solution.

Hannah prayed desperately for a baby, and God answered her; this was easy.

But let's not forget that God is infinite, and His ways are also infinite. Ruth in the Bible experienced God's miraculous blessing many years after being married (ten years of marriage to Mahlon and fewer years with Boaz). The book of Ruth, chapter 4; verse 13 (ESV): *So Boaz took Ruth, and she became his wife. And he went into her, and <u>the LORD gave her conception</u>, and she bore a son.*

His ways are not our ways; therefore, He may choose to build and bless one with children the untraditional way. Today, although man is blessed with the best of science and technology in the field of reproductive endocrinology, it is God who gives life. Man cannot breathe the breath of life into any biological treatment. Many couples have adopted embryos from others who willingly gave them as gifts so that they can experience the joy of pregnancy and parenthood. Some have accepted donated gametes to achieve family, while others adopted babies and children. We are all related by DNA because we are made in God's image.

To women and couples opened to God's infinite ways, I implore you to be open-minded as well because receiving the blessing of a baby may not be through the traditional way as our finite minds may comprehend but may be determined by how desperate and open-minded you can be to God's matchless and masterful plans of realizing that blessing.

So, again I say God alone is God and will never leave His throne. He may place a baby in your arms in an unexpected way. Listen out for His direction and trust His plan.

Pamela Rasheed

CHAPTER 12
MY BACK STORY

Evangelist Ida Mack-Humphrey

As I journey through this desolate terrain of life, making my way toward my eternal abode, I am acutely aware of my human limitations and the necessity of God's assistance and miraculous intervention on my path. The Scriptures have taught me to anchor my faith in God's unwavering and dependable nature. I am convinced that He is entirely trustworthy, without any doubt or hesitation, both now and for all eternity.

The Lord is the priority of my life and the main focus of my trust and worship. So, my love for God overflows with words of praise, even in the midst of difficulty during a very hard and trying time in my life after my son passed on and went home to be with the Lord.

God spoke His word to my heart from (Psalms. 63:3-4) *"Because Your lovingkindness is better than life, My lips shall praise You. Thus, I will bless You while I live; I will lift up my hands in Your name."* Then, I realized my love and devotion to the Lord was alive, real, and eternal. All because His Word is alive and spoke life into my depressed circumstances, which revived me. God promised never to leave me nor never to leave me alone. So, I rejoice in His lovingkindness which is His abundant grace that can carry someone through the valley of the shadow of death into the light of His love and peace.

My ability to worship the Lord grew from my genuine love for Him, who has been my rock in the good and bad seasons of life. The root of my praise sprouted from my knowledge of His unchanging love and devotion for His redeemed children. I learned that by spending quiet time in His presence in prayer. Reading and meditating on His word helped me discover new facets of His character. It also deepened my walk with Him. That is why He deserves all my worship.

There have been some rough roads to cross and some deep valley experiences, and I thought the shadows of death would overshadow me. But I observed how the Lord met my need and showered me with His mercy and compassion. And that experience of His faithfulness and love increased my love and devotion for Him. Now I have learned to continue to praise Him for His abundant provision, comfort, and strength, in times of pain and adversity. It has made me who I am today. My transformation has become my testimony of gratitude for Him making and shaping my life into the image of Christ.

My Psalm
Ida Mack-Humphrey

O my Lord, I trust in thee, for You are my God!
My days are in Your hand;
deliver me and protect me from my enemies
with thy powerful hand and outstretched arms.
Do not let them persecute me.
Make Your face shine upon me and be
gracious unto me.
For thy great mercies are new every morning,
keeping, protecting, and saving me from my enemies.
O how wonderous are You Words to me;
they pour courage and strength deep within
my heart and soul.
So, I hope in Your loving presence,
which has preserved my soul and saved my life
from going down into the pit of destruction, Selah.

Author's Exhortation

It is beyond imagination what the heart and soul of a mother feel and look like at the demise of her son for anyone who has not faced such tragedy. The Evangelist, sister Ida did not go into detail about her immense loss of her only child, her son, but the turmoil she faced is echoed in her Psalm.

When a husband or wife dies, their spouse is called a widower or a widow. When parents die, the children are called father-less, mother-less, or orphans, but when a child dies, there is no word in the dictionary to describe that mother or father. The reason is simple: there are no words. And so, too, no words can do justice in comforting a mom who lives to see death snatches her son away. Astounding!

I am reminded of the Shunamite woman recorded in scriptures in 2 Kings 4:8-37 who did not have many words but said throughout that "it is well." The grief a parent feels when a child goes ahead of them in death is unimaginable, but Evangelist, sister Ida assured her readers that her strength in this challenging time came from the source of her existence, God and His word. She looked to the Word of God for sustenance and testified that holding on to the promises of God gave her the strength and peace she needed to survive.

The Bible calls the Shunamite woman a "great" woman. Before she was a mother, she was a great woman, and without being asked, she found it in her heart to consult her husband about building and furnishing a room in her house for the prophet Elisha so that he could come in and rest whenever he needed to. Unbeknownst to her, God was looking after a matter in her heart. God blessed her with a son. But that son died suddenly at a young age, and the Shunamite woman's words at this time were very limited and her strength enormous. The anguish and sense of helplessness which follow the finality of death can only be quenched by the peace of the Prince of Peace. Only by His grace can someone be constructive, even in tragedy. The Shunammite woman was constructive when she proposed to her husband to build a room and furnish it with a bed, table, stool, and candlestick; now, in this tragedy, she was meticulously constructive; she was on a mission.

She laid her son on the bed of the prophet of God and closed the door. She asked her servant to saddle a donkey and take her to the prophet, Elisha, who had prophesied that she would have this son. She bid her servant to ride on and not to restrain unless she asked him to. People asked her along the way if everything was okay, including Elisha's servant, Gehezi, and her incredible reply was, *"It is well"* (2 Kings 4:26). How could she say that? Her son just died! But this woman was positive in her faith in God. She recognized that the same God that blessed her with a son is the same God that can help her in this tragic time. He is the one to fix it. For some, it may be a means to bring us closer to walk with Him, while for others, He restores and heals.

So, dear reader, if you are faced with such tragedy, know that it is ok to grieve. Also, be encouraged that God has what you need to sustain you. He will bring out good from tragedy because He is God. His Word: His love letter of comfort and sustenance is available to embrace you. Look into It; look to God, and he will see you through one day at a time.

"Be anxious for nothing, but in everything by prayer and supplication, with thanksgiving, let your request be made known to God; and the peace of God, which surpasses all understanding, will guard your hearts and minds through Christ Jesus."
(Philippians 4:6-7).

Pamela Rasheed

CHAPTER 13
Pamela Rasheed's Backstory

A few years ago, I was faced with the challenge of finding a new home after a divorce. Given that I received full custody of my teenage kids and the legal option to sell the marital home and split the proceeds, I chose to relinquish my portion and negotiate to stay there until my younger child began high school. This was granted by the court, and the plan was reasonable for all of us, including my soon-to-be-ex, who gets to keep the home and move back in after all.

The postponement of my relocation served numerous benefits. For one, my son's middle school was conveniently located just across the street from our marital home. Moreover, my ex-spouse was residing in another apartment within the same building, allowing our children to visit him as frequently as they wished. Additionally, my mother and other relatives also resided in the same building, which provided us with a built-in support system. The babysitter's commute would remain the same as it has been since the children were babies, and it was of utmost importance that she remained in her position to maintain the needed stability for the kids while I went to work and school; she took exceptional care of the kids, and we wholeheartedly trusted her.

As the new deadline to relocate drew closer, I became increasingly anxious because I was uncertain about what I really wanted. I couldn't make up my mind about whether to rent or buy a new home or whether to search for an apartment or a house. Additionally, I was unsure whether I should move far away from my current location or remain in the same vicinity. This search became multi-layered and stress-provoking because while the kids had to get used to their father's new life, I needed to be very keen and consider the possibility that they don't feel negated out of his life.

During the search, my kids regularly updated their dad on the challenges we faced for a new home. As a result, my ex-spouse and I reached an agreement where we agreed to a truce. Under this arrangement, my children and I were allowed to remain in the marital home for an extended period, provided that I paid rent to their father. I did for the next two years. The search resumed at the expected time, but I was still conflicted and couldn't fully decide what I truly wanted.

In January 2018, my church was raising funds for a new boiler, and I felt inspired to write a check for a significant amount. With that, I said to God, "Lord, you know I need every dollar at this time should I decide to purchase a house, but I will give this to Your house as a seed offering, and I will believe you to help me to make an informed decision and find a reasonable and convenient place to live because you are my Way-

Maker." I continued my prayer and said, "Lord, I know that I can't outgive you because all that I have belongs to you anyway" I said, "Lord, you know that I don't know what I want, and I haven't been so conflicted in my life" I continued" Lord, you see the houses and apartments that I have seen and how much work the cheaper ones need. You know I do not have a man to fix anything, and I can only compensate with one income, so I am asking you to help me decide". I wrote that check and said, "I give this to you knowing that You are able."

I prayed so sincerely that morning, but then it appeared that all hell broke loose!

By the third week of January, I received an eviction notice from my ex-spouse and his new wife. I was caught off guard by this arrangement, as my ex-spouse collected the rent regularly but did not communicate a specific deadline for when we would need to vacate the property. To say the least, I extended an olive branch and showed much kindness to his new wife, knowing she would be in my children's life somehow. I took her shopping, dining, job interviews, etc., as she was new to the country and English was her second language. I was stunned at their action.

In February, my daughter was involved in a car accident, totaling her car. In March, my high-level nursing job at Columbia University became more stressful as the department tightened its budget in the new year and was unwilling to offer me more than one nursing assistant.

It seemed like all my trouble held a conference and decided to close in on me from every corner, but as I pondered how to navigate these four very unpleasant circumstances and still keep my head above water, so to speak, the Holy Spirit seemed to say *"take heart and stay still because God was up to something."* I reminded myself that "when the enemy shall come in like a flood, the spirit of God will raise up a standard against him and put him to flight" (Isaiah 59:19).

In January of that year, I committed to teaching a course at the Highland church Bible Institute for the first time. The semester was to start in April, but these burdens were weighing heavier, and I thought, "Something has got to give way," so I decided to retract the decision to teach HBI and hand over the Bible course material and lesson structure along with my moral support to my assistant instead. Upon entering the home of Sister Denise (assistant instructor) to discuss the above, she greeted me and retreated quickly to her kitchen to make me a cup of tea as she perceived I was exhausted. At that moment, The Lord showed up again. I heard the voice of God saying, *"I have gone ahead of you to fix that house, do for me what you promised to do, and I will do for you that I will do."* During this encounter with the Lord, it was abundantly clear that I no longer needed to hand over but to teach. God Himself promised to enable me.

While going through this challenging season, I encouraged myself in the Lord and remained calm. The word of the Lord: "*The LORD will cause your enemies who rise against you to be defeated before your face; they shall come out against you one way and flee before you seven ways. The LORD shall command the blessing upon thee in thy storehouses, and in all that thou settest thine hand unto, and he shall bless thee in the land which the LORD thy God giveth thee. (Deuteronomy 28:7,8 KJV)* sealed it for me.

I remembered the lives of Esther and Joseph, how one event led to another, and yet another, that eventually accomplished God's master plan for their lives. I pondered every left, right, and uppercut the enemy seemed to be throwing, but I knew these things would not have happened if God didn't allow them, as with Job in the Bible. And while He allowed the turmoil, I was learning to trust Him and continually encouraged myself.

"For I know the plans I have for you, declares the Lord, plans to prosper you and not to harm you, plans to give you hope and a future."

Jeremiah 29:11

And Hallelujah! One victory led to another and another.

- **Battle #1: WON!**

    The judge threw the eviction case out and said, "A father needs to provide basic needs for his kids, and a roof over their heads is a basic need." And

I could stay in the marital home longer if I wanted.

- **Battle #2: WON!**

The car insurance paid more than the car was worth, and my daughter was able to get a Lexus.

- **Battle #3: WON!**

A job recruiter contacted me about a new job and made me an offer I could not refuse, albeit I wasn't planning to leave Columbia.

- **Battle #4: WON!**

It became crystal clear that I must buy and not rent a house and not an apartment. No more was I conflicted in my mind as to what I really wanted.

The HBI Spring Semester 2018 started on April 15th and concluded on June 17th, when I resumed my search for a new home. I fell in love with a house of which my offer was rejected. I cried for over an hour.

How quickly I seemed to forget that I was on a winning streak (battles #1-#5).

I placed the matter before the Lord. I said this prayer: 'Lord, you know that I like that house. Lord, you know I am doing this single-handedly, and the price is right. Lord, you know that I don't have a man to fix anything, so I need a house that's move-in ready, and this house is the one. Lord, I know a homosexual spirit lives there, but you can take care of that. So, please let the people whose offer was accepted stop liking the house and back off so that my offer can be accepted". Yes, this was my prayer.

I felt like God did not hear a word from that prayer. But I continued still, this time on my knees, and said, "Lord, you know my taste and how much I like nice things; I like this house, but if it is not your will, so be it. And if it is not your will, then it means You have something better in store. So, if you have something better in store, please hurry up"!

But the Holy Spirit reminded me of David in the Bible of how he killed a bear, a lion, and the giant Goliath. The battle belongs to the Lord.

Well indeed! God was working it out as He promised while I stood in Sister Denise's house that day.

On April 19th, this house I currently reside in was listed for sale as a foreclosure. A builder purchased it on May 1st and subsequently conducted a complete renovation, replacing everything from the roof to the basement with brand-new items. The house was then listed for sale on July 25th. Following the successful conclusion of the Spring semester and amidst six competing offers, my offer on this house was accepted on August 2nd. I proceeded to sign the contract on

August 17th and was able to close on the house in less than two months.

This house is more than I imagined. It was completely redone with all modern amenities, including a huge yard, a new landscape in the front, an office, and a terrace on the roof. While the initial mortgage company caused a delay in the process, God showed up yet again and directed me to a banker who was my Sunday school student in Guyana many years ago. He waived the amortization fee worth over five thousand dollars. The time from the contract to closing was so swift that I had to ask the realtor, banker, lawyer, and seller to slow down!

God has a great sense of humor. I was reminded of my prayer asking God to "hurry up"!

On December 8th, 2018, as I was hosting a Housewarming thanksgiving service, I remembered the prayer I prayed as I gave the seed offering in January (I had literally forgotten about it all year). I remembered God's promise on March 31st in sister Denise's house. I remembered that prayer I prayed for God to "hurry up!"

The housewarming service was made even more special by the celebration of His faithfulness. The invitation to my friends and relatives read *"A Celebration of His Faithfulness."*

This personal Psalm of Amazement at God's Faithfulness in an uncertain season of my life.

Pamela Rasheed

A Psalm of God's Amazing Faithfulness

Pamela Rasheed

Oh Lord, You have blown my mind away!
It is all Your doing — only You.
Your faithfulness is more than I could fathom.

When I faced that uncertain season
filled with doubts and feelings of despair,
You set me on a course and blew my mind away.
It is You who did it beyond my expectations.
You blew my mind away, and I was in awe.

Name the ways I may praise you, and I will;
because when my eyes beheld your perfect
work and how you put it all together.
I am short for words fitting for Your praise.
It is only you, and forever I will be grateful.

Oh! Why did I despair and try to fathom
the end from the beginning?
My finite mind was no match for your infinite greatness.
Oh, how easy it was to put my trust in me,

Blessed In The Detours Of Life

but to no avail until I gave it to You, the infinite one!

You have done so much for me before;
I remembered, yet I only see through
my little vision of Your greatness.
Now, I magnify You and give You praise!
You heard the cries from deep within
And blew my mind away
with your amazing grace and faithfulness.

You are the One and no other!
Selah

When it was all done, it and set before mine eyes;
I stood in awe and repented of my self-trust
and limited view of who You,
the one who alone knew the end even before it began.
It was all your handiwork; You are the one. Selah.

You stayed true to your word
when the enemy came in like a flood.
You set up that standard and wrought the magnificent end;
You blew my mind with your faithfulness.
So, name more ways that I may praise you, and I will.

Co-Author Exhortation

In life, we will, at some point or another, experience ups and downs; the bitter and the sweet; good and bad, but it's important that we understand this reality so we can be prepared for some of life's challenges.

As a child of God and people of faith, we have heard about or read Psalms 34, where the great Psalmist David said that many are the afflictions of the righteous, but The Lord will deliver us out of them all.

Despite the fact that scripture warns us about the reality and possibility of such challenges, we do not look forward to any bitter experience, nor do we welcome any affliction coming in our direction. The truth is that sometimes we will have a mountain-top experience of pure joy, satisfaction, and happiness. Then, suddenly, we can find ourselves drowning and sinking as if the boat has flipped upside down. Sometimes it's slowly taking in water, and other times, we are blindsided by the surfacing storm.

Many can testify that life is not a bed of roses alone; we will occasionally experience the sting of thorns connected to the roses.

What's vital is that we never forget The Word of The Lord because it is the manual that provides us with instructions on how to deal with the thorns. God's word is our GPS (God's positioning system) when we feel lost and frustrated in our detours of life. God says He is still there and will redirect and take us back on course.

Even when we can't trace Him, we must never forget to trust Him. We are all flawed beings who are easily distracted, sidetracked, or end up going in the wrong way.

No matter how the ups and downs, bitter or sweet, bad or good, are, never allow your mind tostop you from seeking The Lord for advice on his master plan for you. The Lord never wants us to suffer in silence. His will is not for any of us to feel lost or to be spiritually and physically drained and depleted. He's our comforter and the only one who has the answer for every problem we will ever experience. We must always fight within to hear the voice of The Holy Spirit.

We must always do our best to forgive others of their trespasses against us. Forgiveness frees us and prevents bitterness from building up. It's not an option; it's a requirement if we want to experience God's best for us. The wonderful thing about The Lord is that He hears our hearts even before we speak the words and honors a spirit of humility and forgiveness.

I'm reminded of the story of Daniel, in chapter 9:10, who had a love and reverence for God in- spite of the imperfections around him. Daniel sought God for forgiveness and loved the Lord with all of his heart as he prayed and cried out to God for answers and help. The wonderful thing about this story is that God dispatched an angel to answer Daniel's prayer the moment he thought it before it became words. How awesome is it that God hears our heart before our words and sometimes instead of our words? It's the sincere heart that moves God. The Heart of Prayer, The Non-verbal longing for God and whatever He has to offer us in our time of need and desperation.

God said that Daniel was highly esteemed, and He felt the same way about us. When we are faithful in our love and reverence to God, He will be faithful to us. He knows our needs and struggles because He is The Alpha and The Omega. He's an Omnipotent, Omniscient, Omnipresent, and Immutable God. He knows all, see's all, and is all-powerful. He's the same yesterday, today, and forever more. Yes, He's all of that and more. God will touch us and give us strength when we are weak.

God will always honor sincere prayers; it's not about what we did or did not do but about our sincere conversation with Him, our creator who always looks forward to communicating with us and answering us.

Also, be reminded that the scripture tells us in 1 Corinthians 10 that with every trial and temptation in life, God will never allow us to be tempted more than we can bear, and more importantly, He will always make a way of escape for us. He will provide that ram in the bush for us. He will send a safety net, a parachute, and a rope to pull us out of the quicksand.

The quiet whisper of the Holy Spirit will bring back to our remembrance what we need to remember before the clock strikes midnight. He's the chariot with adorned majestic horses, which will get us back on track. He will remove the scales from our eyes and melt and dissolve the hardened plaque that blocks our path. He will re-open the closed lid we hold so tightly to. God understands freedom and timing but not our desired time frame or our understanding of time. God's timing differs significantly from ours, but he will always free us.

When we are blinded by closed eyes or afraid to look, God will always open our eyes with His supernatural Trifocal lenses equipped with multiple powers because He is a Triune God who will always allow His children to experience a clear vision and path toward deliverance. Jesus holds the key to the cell of our minds, and we only need to have the desire to be free. All we must do is thirst for the living water Jesus offers, and we will be satisfied by Him and thirst no more.

The Lord hears our prayers, calms our fears, and collects our tears. He will give you double for your trouble. He will blow your mind and be glorified on the earth. Never stop praying, Never stop trusting, and Never stop believing. Fight to be free. John 8:36 says Christ will set you free, and you will be free indeed. Selah

Doctor, Chaplain, Cheryl James

CHAPTER 14

Kathleen Smith's Backstory

Several years ago, on a Friday in May, an event occurred that left me shaken. I was working at a bank that followed a shift system where the workday cuts off at 2 pm. At this time, we would balance and rebook the computer systems, and any remaining transactions would be carried over to the following day's work. In banking, Friday evenings are the busiest of all, but on this particular Friday, I felt ecstatic because my vacation would officially begin at 6 pm.

After signing off at 2 pm, I went out for lunch, unaware that Satan, my adversary, was about to stir up trouble. Although I had no intention of entering any further data that day, I was eager to provide customer service, a task that I thoroughly enjoyed. However, sometime later, I heard someone was "out" of $40,000. I was relieved that it wasn't my ID! I then signed out and went next door to the mall. Unexpectedly, my friend came looking for me, saying, "It's your ID that keyed in on the next workday." "No way!" I said. "I did not key anything in at all." I handed over everything already and was ready to go to Guyana for a much-needed vacation.

That weekend was the worst time for me. I was asking God, "Why me?" I was a Catholic then at that time, I prayed, "God, you know I'm an honest person; why would you allow someone to set me up? I would never steal and damage my character for that. Please have mercy on me and expose the person behind such a cruel deed! Let it just be an honest human or system error.

God is good! He isolated the entry so what the enemy meant to get mixed up with a whole day's work, and therefore hard to find, became crystal clear.

Turned out that a coworker keyed in the fake deposit and then had her boyfriend rush to withdraw the funds before anyone could figure it out. I thank God another co-worker from the other branch knew our staff and felt something wasn't right. That co-worker took immediate action by calling my branch to confirm the transaction.

By Monday, the police had interviewed all the workers and the boyfriend of the suspected co-worker. Thank God people knew I was honest. The thief told her boyfriend to say that he had conducted the deposit transaction with Kathy. The lie that they planned to cover up the theft was crystal clear because I was off that Monday morning.

When he came to the bank to identify the person that allegedly assisted him with the fake deposit transaction, he asked a worker to show him who Kathy was. As God would have it, they showed him the other Kathy, who also worked there, so he identified her as the person instead.

I told them I would cancel my trip because I didn't want to be embarrassed at the airport for something I didn't do. But they smiled and said no, we have proof you didn't do it. You can go enjoy your vacation.

The interesting thing is that someone told me to read Psalm 55. I couldn't say it because how do you pray to God to kill your enemy? Didn't the bible say don't kill?

For months, no one could explain what it really meant, not even my priest. During Thanksgiving, a friend invited us to their church, where a visiting Minister from another church was preaching about David and Ahithophel. He dissected Psalm 55, and Wow! God had a greater plan for me. My spiritual eye was opened, and from then on, that became my home church because they always explained the Word of God clearly and with understanding.

God used my low place and brought me out as only He can! Oh, the Victory we have in Jesus! And Salvation. John 3:16-18

Psalm – A Low moment

- Kathleen Smith -

I need Thee, oh God
How I need Thee
Don't forsake me.
Oh God, my soul screams within me!
My heart cries out to You
For I am anguished within my soul.

Oh God, Thou art mine Refuge
Please do not be silent.
Attend unto my cause, oh Lord.
Be gracious, be merciful.
to your humble servant, Your daughter
Remember me, oh Father!

Judge me, oh God, and they that doeth inequity.
Measure us, oh Lord, in search of justice.
Hold them accountable for their wicked deeds.
Cut off their wretchedness towards me.
Hide me, oh Lord, in Thy bosom!
Remove their evil counsel from my situation.
Confuse and confound the enemy.

Wash all bitterness from me, dear Lord
Restore me and all that the enemy has stolen from me.
Comfort me, Sweet Jesus.
Shelter me with Your saving grace.
You are a glorious and always faithful God!

I give Thee honor and glory!
All praise unto You, my Father.
Forgive me for all my trespasses.
Change my disposition,
Lord, do not tarry!
Preserve me for thy loving kindness sake.
Hallelujah!

Author's Exhortation

Psalm 55 in the Bible is a psalm of lament by Kind David when he was betrayed by his trusted friend and Ahithophel and feared for his safety yet again. David expressed his emotions by referring to his heart as being "in anguish." Yet, while he was overwhelmed by horror and stated that he was restless, he still cast his cares on the LORD because he knew that God would sustain him.

But as David lamented in these situations and called upon God to rescue him, he also prayed, *"Let death seize upon them, and let them go down quick into hell: for wickedness is in their dwellings, and among them"* (v 15). This is a prayer of imprecation against his enemies. How can one pray for the destruction and death of others? Why should this even be in the Bible?

The Psalms of the Bible are not only rich with beautiful poetry, adoration, praises, and joys, but there is also sorrow, laughter, lamentations, and imprecations.

So, what is an imprecation? It is a curse that invokes misfortune or death upon someone perceived as an enemy. In the Old Testament and the Psalms, there are imprecations in which the authors call down calamity, destruction, and God's anger and judgment on his enemies.

At the heart of these imprecations is the yearning for justice over wickedness and unrighteousness. "Rise up,

LORD, confront them, bring them down; with your sword, rescue me from the wicked" (Psalm 17:13).

There are over a dozen imprecatory Psalms in the Holy Bible, which point to Jesus and His enemy, Satan. The entire Old Testament depicted Jesus, and Jesus said that the Old Testament is still valid and binding and that he did not come to destroy the Law but to fulfill it (Matthew 5: 17-20).

So, how does Jesus fulfill the imprecations in the Psalms? He did so through His death and resurrection. He destroyed His enemy! He conquered hell and death, and we ought to rejoice in our Salvation; He saves us and places His righteousness upon us, justifying us by His Blood before His Father.

Now we know who the real enemy is, and it is not one another. The New Testament does not encourage believers to pray imprecations. The Apostle Paul encourages believers saying, "Bless those who persecute you; bless and curse not" (Rom 12:14). Satan is the enemy whom Jesus overcame for us. And as we tarry on this pilgrim journey, let us remember to whom our prayers of imprecations should be directed.

Kathleen Smith

*For we wrestle not against flesh and blood,
but against principalities, against powers,
against the rulers of the darkness of this world,
against spiritual wickedness in high places*

(Ephesians 6:12).

--Pamela Rasheed--

CHAPTER 15

A Call To Worship and Praise!

Evangelist Ida Mack-Humphrey

(1

Born To Worship God

Many Christians are missing the genuine and sacred offering of ourselves and our worship of God. The world is watching the church today, and if we profess faith in Jesus Christ and fail to show His love and compassion to others, we miss the mark. We are obligated to stand up for the truth and contend for the faith when necessary. Rather than simply reading a

Bible, the world desires to witness the embodiment of its teachings in our Christ-like behavior. Our responsibility as individuals whom He has called from darkness into His glorious light is to showcase this transformation through our conduct. We join the army of true saints when God's purposes in Christ become clear to us. We join them when we begin to worship God because of who He is.

Jesus, born of a virgin, suffered under Pontius Pilate, died on the cross, and rose from the grave to make worshipers out of sinful men, and He has done it all through His amazing grace. And, as the recipients, we must learn the meaning and the delight of worshiping Him and prioritize it above everything else.

God is calling us back to that for which He created us: to worship Him and enjoy Him forever! Then out of our deep worship, we can do His work effectively. We will not spend our time with carnal or worldly religious projects if we are among the worshipers. All the examples of godly men and women in the Bible illustrate that joyful, devoted, and reverent worship is the normal employment of mortal human beings. Every glimpse that is given to us of heaven and of God's created beings is always a glimpse of worship, rejoicing, and praise because of who God is.

The apostle John in Revelation 4:10-11 gives us a portrait of created beings around the throne of God. John explains the occupation of all the elders in this manner. *"The twenty-four elders fall before Him who sits on the throne and worship Him who lives forever and ever, and cast their crowns before the throne, saying: "You are worthy, O Lord, to receive glory and honor and power; For You created all things, And by Your will, they exist and were created."* All of this is revealed to us in the Word of God. Therefore, if anyone on this earth feels bored, turned off, or refuses to worship their creator, they are not ready for heaven. We are saved by grace through faith and redeemed by the blood of Jesus so that we might worship and adore our creator. God has given us the gift of Salvation so that we might be, individually and personally, vibrant children of God, loving God with all our hearts, minds, and souls and worshiping Him in the beauty of His holiness.

The Holy Spirit, the third person of the God head, does not operate by a set formula or a person's preconceived idea or agenda. The Holy Spirit of God comes among us with His anointing, and we become worshippers as we genuinely express our praise and adoration to the God of all grace, all love, all mercy, and all truth. And we may not be quiet enough to please everyone.

In the book of Luke (19:37-40), on that first Palm Sunday, the disciples and the crowd began to rejoice and praise God; they were shouting aloud and saying, "*Blessed is the King who comes in the name of the Lord!' Peace in heaven and glory in the highest!"* And the Pharisees wanted

Jesus to keep the crowd quiet. But He said, *"I tell you that if these should keep silent, the stones would immediately cry out."* This was the time of their worship; they were united in praises to God. The worship of the saints of God in the body of Christ has often been a little loud and noisy. The beautiful part of worship is that it prepares and enables you to focus on the important things that must be done for God. Be attentive to this thought; practically every great deed done in the church of Christ all the way back to the time of the Apostle Paul was done by people blazing with the radiant worship of their God.

It is important for us to understand and discover why we were born. God had a specific purpose in mind when He created the human race. It was distinctly the will of God that men and women created in His image would desire fellowship with Him above all else. God's plan was to be a perfect fellowship based on adoring worship of our creator and sustainer of all things. We were made to worship. The shorter Catechism asks a searching question; "What is the chief end of man?" In response, the author of the Westminster Confession wrote, "Man's chief and highest end is to glorify God and to fully enjoy Him forever." When we love God with all our hearts, we are the closest we will ever be in this world to living in God's eternal kingdom.

God created man so that when He looked at him, He might see more of His own glory reflected in him than in the starry skies above. That is our end. We were created to worship, glorify, and have Him as our God forever. But when Adam and Eve sinned, the mirror was dimmed and blurred. When God would look at sinful man, He could no longer see His own glory. That disobedient man had become sinful, failing to fulfill God's ultimate purpose of his creation to worship Him in the beauty and splendor of holiness.

Thank God man wasn't written off by his creator, and this is wonderful news for humans in that the supreme creator, God of the universe, did not give up on us. He still wanted that relationship with the man that mirrors His glory. He still wanted His people to enjoy Him forever. For this purpose, He sent His only begotten Son, Jesus, into the world to redeem us back to Him. When Jesus walked the earth, He was the reflection of the glory of God. When He looked at Mary's Son, He saw a reflection of Himself. Jesus said, "When you have seen Me, you have seen the Father. In other words, He was saying, "When you see me, you are seeing my Father's glory. Jesus came to finish the work of redemption He has been given to do. God was glorified in His Son, even at His death on the cross. The angels rejoiced in heaven because the sinful man had been redeemed.

Jesus, the way, the truth, and the life, has pardoned and forgiven lost sinners who repent. And now, since His resurrection, He is seated at the Father's right hand. He has been interceding for us to return to our original purpose of being mirrors and reflectors of God's glory. As a result, we who are born again ought to worship, praise, and adore the God who not only created us, but recreated us in Christ Jesus our Lord.

(2)

Understanding Your Call

The phrase: *"Oh, that men would praise the lord for His goodness, and for His wonderful works to the children of men,"* is repeated throughout Psalm 107. The Psalmist reflects on the depth of God's care for His people in the wilderness when they cried out for His help. As a result, he calls the people of God to thank Him for His faithful love and care for them, the very ones in covenant with Him. Such wonderful knowledge should cause us, who are redeemed and in covenant through the shed blood of Jesus, to praise Him for His mighty deliverance in our times of trouble.

As Christians, we are described in several ways: a royal priesthood, a holy nation, and a special people, not based on our own merits but through Jesus Christ. We have access directly to the throne room, the Holy of Holies. We do not need a high priest to perform our atonement or represent us to God.

We are also a people of His own possession; we belong to Him.

Along with our new identity in Christ, we are to live a new lifestyle to the glory of The Father. A life that proclaims the praises of Him who has called us out of darkness into His marvelous light. In other words, we are Christ's ambassadors with the task of sharing the message of His love. The world ought to see what a marvelous God He is through demonstration of the life we live.

Another term that describes our Christian life is being a "Christ follower." A follower chooses the path of action. Our trust in Christ develops as we abide in Him and discover the beauty of His character, love, and plan for our lives. We obey Him because we love Him. We say *"yes"* to His will when it's difficult, *"yes"* when it's unpopular, and *"yes"* even when it may cause us heartache. Our call is to always serve Him. God wants His children not to be mere observers but to be active participants in His kingdom work. We are called to use our gifts and talents to do our part within the body of Christ. As we fulfill our call to emulate Jesus, the one who has delivered us from the kingdom of darkness and redeemed us, let us then proclaim aloud with worship and praise that the Lord has done great things for us, whereof we are glad.

(3)

Executing Your Action

"Oh come, let us worship and bow down; Let us kneel before the Lord our Maker For He is our God, And we are the people of His pasture, And the sheep of His hand..." (Ps. 95:6-7). The psalmist calls God's people to demonstrate their submission to Him by bowing down before Him. A posture symbolizing the recognition of His sovereignty. As the sheep depend on their shepherd to protect and provide for them, we, as God's people in His pasture, look to Him for our daily provisions and sustenance.

We must think about the Lord our God, who is able to help us live victoriously in this pilgrim journey no matter what we face. And because of God's love for us, we are more than conquerors through Christ. As we come before His presence with worship and adoration just for who He is, we bow down and bless His Holy Name.

We must also learn to pause and meditate on the attributes of the Agape love He exhibits, a love not based on our worth or merit but on who He is. He is sovereign and always in total control. He is omnipotent and has all power. He is omnipresent, present everywhere, all of Him and all the time. Our God is omniscient, He knows everything. He is truthful; whatever He says is true, and He can't lie. And He is holy! All of which should cause us to humble ourselves and be in awe of His majesty's mighty presence. It's important to praise Him for His mighty acts of salvation and remember all the ways He has helped us yesterday, today, and will forever if we trust Him. He is our way-maker!

As we open God's eternal Word and read about His mighty, marvelous works, let us each learn to cultivate an attitude of gratitude for His presence and power in our lives as He was with the saints of old. The Bible says, "What then shall we say to these things? If God is for us, who can be against us? (Rom. 8:31).

Nothing can stand against a child of God who walks in obedience to His will. Therefore, we put our trust and hope in the God of all creation, who is mighty in power, perfect in wisdom, and abounding in unfailing love.

(4)

He Is Light

"Let all that I am praise the Lord; may I never forget the good things he does for me." (Ps. 103:2 NLT) There's no one like the true and living God. The Bible equates God with light and light with holiness. (Jn. 1:5) "God is light, and in Him, there is no darkness." "Who alone is immortal and who lives in unapproachable light, whom no one has seen or can see. To him be honor and might forever…" (1 Timothy. 6:16). Scripture refers to Christ who is holy, blameless, pure, and set apart from sinners. Which is why born-again Christians praise and worship the God who created us in His own image and likeness. And re-created us in His Son.

Now we're heirs and joint heirs with our great and mighty God.

Jesus told His followers to pray; "Our Father who art in heaven, hollowed be thy name." (Matt. 6:9) This is how we must approach God as our Father who loves us dearly and desires only what is best for us; while always regarding Him with profound reverence. As our awe of God grows, our fear of life will diminish. God's greatness is unsearchable. Having a big view of God translates into big courage. Because our God can do the exceedingly and abundantly, above all, we can ask or think. He can help when cancer strikes. He's there when our family is in trouble. He can help when we have no way to pay our bills. You need an awesome God who enlarges your faith and blows your mind with His power. May we never forget the good things He does for us. He forgives, heals all, redeems us from ultimate death, and crowns us with His love and tender mercies. He fills our mouths with good things, and our youth is renewed like the eagles. Every good gift comes from Him. He has freely given that glorious inheritance in heaven and secured our Salvation through the death and resurrection of His only begotten son, and this is why we bless the Lord with all that's within us, we ought to bless His holy name forever!

(5)

Ultimate Occupation of the Saints of God

"I will extol (Praise) You, my God, O King; And I will bless Your name forever and ever. Every day I will bless You, And I will praise Your name forever and ever. Great is the Lord, and greatly to be praised; And His greatness is unsearchable. One generation shall praise Your works to another and shall declare Your mighty acts. I will meditate on the glorious splendor of Your majesty, And on Your wondrous works. Men shall speak of the might of Your awesome acts, And I will declare Your greatness. They shall utter the memory of Your great goodness and shall sing of Your righteousness. The Lord is gracious and full of compassion, Slow to anger and great in mercy." (Ps. 145:1-8).

When I think about who God is, I'm sometimes left speechless. I have spent many times on my knees pondering and meditating on Him, and I found myself crying. Why? Because of how awesome He is. Because He answers our prayers and has been good, gracious, and forgiving repeatedly. Because He makes His presence known and allows us to converse with Him in prayer. God assures us in the Bible of His powerful, unshakeable, eternal, and unconditional love.

"For God is love." (1 John. 1:8). Therefore, how could we ever choose not to worship, follow, obey, be guided by, and love Him in return?

Regardless of what we imagine, it's important that we look at the Scripture to see what the Lord says about Himself. In it, we learn what He is like, what He loves, and how He relates to us. In the book of Isaiah, the 40th chapter, we read how it centers on God's greatness and majesty and describes Him as far superior to creation. Even the most powerful earthly ruler is nothing in comparison. The Father's wisdom and might reign over everything. Compared to the Lord, the nations of the earth are "like a drop from a bucket, and are regarded as a speck of dust on the scales. He is also more powerful than lifeless man-made idols that cannot answer prayers or empower us. We read that the Lord is above and beyond this world. He's transcending. (Isa. 40:22) It states, "It is He who sits above the circle of the earth, and its inhabitants are like grasshoppers, who stretches out the heavens like a curtain And spreads them out like a tent to dwell in."

He is El-Elyon the Lord most high. Who is above the heavens and the stars, calling them all by name; because of the greatness of His might and the strength of His power, not one of them is missing. The planets, the galaxies, the moon, and the sun are all in order. We can never take God's greatness for granted because He is a source of comfort for all who take refuge in Him. The Lord is immeasurably beyond us in all ways, yet He says in (Isa. 57:15) "I dwell in a high and holy place, and also with the contrite (sorry, penitent) and lowly of spirit." Also, we read in Ps. 51: 16-17, "For You do not desire sacrifice, or else I would give it; You do not delight in burnt offering. The sacrifices of God are a broken spirit, A broken and a contrite heart— These, O God, You will not despise.") If you are a Christian, He's your refuge, sustainer, and protector. Why, because you have been loved and chosen by God.

God provides us with comfort and strength for life: When we dwell on and think about some of His great amazing attributes (Traits, qualities, power, characteristics).

(1) God is Omnipresent (present everywhere, He's universal) – Even when you feel isolated or friendless, you're not alone. (The songwriter said, No, never alone no never alone. He promises never to leave me, no never alone.) God is a loving Father who invites us into a close personal relationship with Him. And because He is everywhere, we never have to face any trial, temptation, or difficulty alone. We are always within His perfect care and kept in His presence every single moment of our lives.

(2) God's understanding is infinite (Vast, endless, limitless) – He knows everything, including your feelings of loneliness, hurt, grief, and discouragement, and knows what your needs are. You may not

understand all that's going on in your life, but the Lord knows and will give you the strength, comfort, and guidance you need. Jesus said (Matt.7:7-8) ask, seek, and knock, that's a form of praying to Him. Why? Because where God finds a praying heart, you will find a prayer-hearing God, and He shall give thee an answer of peace.

(3) The LORD Never Changes as we read in (Mal. 3:6) "For I am the Lord, I do not change...." The unchanging of His essential nature and character is called the immutability of God. He is immutable. People change, time change, seasons change, our circumstances change, but God is consistent and faithful. He is compassionate, gracious, slow to anger, and abounds in faithful love and truth. (Song: Great is Thy faithfulness, O God my Father, There is no shadow of turning with Thee Thou changest not, Thy compassions, they fail not As Thou hast been, Thou forever will be.) As a result, we (His children) have received grace rather than what we deserve. Since His character is constant, you and I can always trust that He will be faithful, gracious, and merciful to us in every situation. Jesus is the same yesterday, today, and forever. He will not turn anyone away who comes to Him; (Jn. 6:37) "... the one who comes to Me I will by no means cast out." God wants a relationship with all His human creation so we will not perish but have everlasting

life with Him now and in eternity. So, if you don't know Jesus, the Son of God who is the way, the truth, and life, I ask you to accept Him today, and He promises to save, deliver, and present you faultless before His father with great joy!

CHAPTER 16

Reverend Brenda Collier

The Back Story

My story has to do with a dream. A dream that has been with me for a long time and still haunts me today.

I love God even though I was raised in a home where the Bible, Jesus Christ, and the church were not mentioned. The Lord made Himself real to me as a young child by appearing to me in a dream, demonstrating His great love and magnificent power. Beyond anything else, this vision secured my faith in God because, through this experience, I knew that God was real and that Jesus was the Almighty God.

As I awoke, the manifestation of the Lord's presence lingered with me, something I thought everyone in the world experienced. The only way I know how to describe the sweetness of His presence is one word: LOVE! Through this visitation came the revelation that God could do anything. If I enquired something from Him, He would meet my every need. He is not just loving, but He is LOVE Himself. He showed me that all I needed to do was ask, and it would be given. He is magnificent.

Through the years, I had a deep yearning to continue to find this wonderful God, and this longing was answered when a neighbor got permission to take me to church. Upon arriving at the church, I entered the empty sanctuary. I quickly drew myself to the altar, where I knelt to seek the Lord and pray.

While I was on my knees, I heard the back door open. As I looked up, a military soldier was standing in the doorway. He was on crutches, and it appeared as if one leg was partially missing. I gasped and returned to pray, and I said: "Father, I know YOU can do anything! Please heal that soldier. Please, Lord, it hurts me to see him walking on those crutches. The next time I see that man, Father, I want to see Him whole, standing on his two feet."

Some time passed, and once again, my neighbor took me to church. I was so elated to be there, and once again, I ran to the altar to talk to God. As my knees hit the hard floor, the door was pushed open. When I turned around to see who was there, I was mesmerized, it was that soldier, and behold, he was standing on his two feet.

Witnessing this phenomenon was life-changing because it confirmed my faith in the One whose Presence abided with me. I uttered something like this: "I knew YOU could do it, Father. Thank you for healing that man. I love YOU, and I will always love You because You answered my prayer."

This affirmation of God answering prayer made me commit to praying and believing God for anything.

During the early years of my adulthood, I found a church where the Gospel was preached, the Bible was revered, and they had a Bible school. I enrolled, and I began my journey to study God's Word. I made many friends. One friend is key to my story because her pain, suffering, and loss brought me to a significant turning point in my relationship with the Lord.

She was married to a wonderful man; however, they were having difficulty starting a family. After her third miscarriage, another friend and I visited her to bring comfort during the darkest period of her life. Together, we ministered to her, prayed, read scripture, and sang songs of praise to the Lord. Yet, no matter what we did, the pain of this last miscarriage seemed to end her hopes and dreams of ever becoming a mother. The three of us sobbed because, although only one of us was experiencing the heartbreaking loss of the hope of motherhood at that time, we all three saw that possibility dwindling.

The doctor told her that her best option was adoption and not trying to get pregnant again. He told her that her body was too frail and pregnancy could be life-threatening. This was devastating for her, but she began to rebuild her faith again by adopting a puppy.

However, the turn of events came about nine months after the loss of their third baby. I received a call and was told she had delivered a healthy baby girl. I could not believe it, but I discovered that she had kept it a secret after she learned she was pregnant. When she learned she had conceived, she did not tell a soul except her husband. Moreover, our second friend announced that she, too, was expecting a baby. I could not get over how the Lord also turned things around for her; she conceived and gave birth to a healthy baby girl.

My mind was baffled.

I went to bed that night with my mind still milling over the entire matter. I fell asleep and had a dream. It was another dream with that visitation, and it still boggles my mind to this day.

The Dream: There were thousands upon thousands of people standing on a sandy beach. Suddenly, an ice cream truck appeared. It was the kind of ice cream truck where the children gathered around the open window, placed orders, and received their cold, creamy delights. However, Jesus also appeared, and He was standing at the open window, wearing a very long flowing white robe. A Shadowy figure inside the truck was gathering the ingredients and making the delectable treats, and then He would hand them directly to Jesus. Then in turn, Jesus would hand them out to everyone who was waiting. A chocolate fudgsicle would be handed out the window, and Jesus would take it and pass it on. "Yum, I said to myself; I wish Jesus would have given me that fudgsicle! Doesn't Jesus know that I love fudgsicles?" Next, it would be a banana split. "Me, me, Lord Jesus – I know it's rather big, but I can eat that delicious banana split." Next, there were milkshakes, ice cream cones, hot fudge sundaes, blizzards, sodas, you name it, everything your heart desired. Then, finally, the Shadowy figure dusted off His hands as if to say that is all for today. When I looked around, everyone was enjoying themselves. Everyone had received some goody from Jesus out of that ice cream truck. I was baffled because it appeared as though Jesus had forgotten me. I was standing so close to Him that I was lost within the folds of His long flowing gown. Maybe Jesus didn't see me, so I stepped out from the folds of His robes, looked up, and asked, "Jesus, where is MY ice cream? Did YOU not see me? Lord, I love fudgsicles. Couldn't I have just a fudgsicle!" With eyes full of love, and a voice as tender as possible, Jesus said: "Daughter, you will have to wait." The tears in my eyes began to overflow because I could not understand, nonetheless, I trusted His wisdom.

We began to walk together; Jesus held my hand as we treaded a long uphill road. Suddenly, I spotted a very exquisite ice cream parlor. "Aha!" I thought, "My ice cream will come from this fancy ice cream parlor." Although that very cheap ice cream from the truck would have sufficed, I will eat the fancy kind. Okay Jesus, let's go inside. But much to my surprise, when we went inside, everyone from the beach scene was there, still eating their frozen treats from Jesus. The Shadowy figure was also there, but he was behind the counter handing out sweets this time. He would grab a fist full of individually wrapped candy and hand them over to Jesus. It appeared that when each person would lick their ice cream, Jesus would hand them candy. The candy seemed to be something like Jolly Ranchers. Some would get one Jolly Rancher, and others may get two or even three.

In the meantime, I was pressed up against Jesus, lost, once again within the folds of His garment. "That is why He didn't give me anything. He can't see me. "Yoo-Hoo Jesus, I'm right here! Yoo- Hoo, don't You see me?" This time, however, I just looked up at Him with tears streaming down my face. And, although I did not audibly say it this time, I just looked up at Him as if to say: "Gee, Jesus, can't I even get a Jolly Rancher?" But even though I did not voice my question, it was as if He read my mind and answered, "Daughter, I said you have to wait." (Dream Ended)

At this point, I woke up and was more frustrated and confused than I was before I fell asleep. Just like when Jesus appeared to me in the first visitation, I knew this dream was from Him. I knew there was a message for me. I could not comprehend why others were not only enjoying their ice creams but also receiving Jolly Ranchers. Although at the time, I did not realize that my faith was being tested. I seriously began to believe Jesus didn't really love me. I spent many years baffled by the idea that I was in love with a God who did not love me. How could this possibly be?

A deep ache began to take hold. How can I be so wrong about this when the Scriptures say, "God is love" and that "God so loved the world"?

Jesus even said; "Greater love has no man than this, that a man lay down his life for His friends." (John 15:13). And Jesus did lay down His life for us. This verse brought me back to reality because that was a demonstration of love I could not deny. Jolly Rancher or no Jolly Rancher, Jesus laid His life down and raised it back up again, just as He said. He does exactly what He says. Therefore, trusting Him and what He said about loving me was a proven fact. An empty tomb says it all! It was not based on what He has given to others. His love is based on what He has accomplished on Calvary. On Calvary, He gave all of us His all.

A Psalm of God's Love Demonstrated to Me

Reverend Brenda Collier

I love Thee oh my God, my strength,
For YOU alone have stood by my side,
In times of deep trouble and overwhelming sorrow,
YOU comforted me with Your spoken Word.

Sorrows came upon me and almost destroyed my soul,
But YOU rescued me.
In my distress, I cried out to You,
You are my strength Jehovah,
You are my abiding strength.
You answer prayers
You turn darkness into light
You are with the broken-hearted

Even in seasons of night
You were there with me in the days of my youth,
You led me, guided me, and sheltered me from harm.
I find myself at home in Your magnificent Arms.
And when heaven and earth may pass away
It is on YOUR WORD I must stay.

Pamela Rasheed

You have given me life,
It's abundant, it's true.
There is no greater friend
or gift Greater than You.
I love Thee, oh my God, my strength.
You are a God of wisdom and the God of great might,
In You I find the Way, Truth, and Life.
Even though my mind may be in a daze,
You are perfect in all Your ways.
Therefore, on You I will WAIT.
In perfect surrender, On Thee I will WAIT.

Author's Exhortation

God speaking to his people through dreams dates to ancient times, but this method is still very real today. As believers, God's messages to us through dreams can be interpreted clearly but there are times when dreams hold mysteries that can sometimes be baffling. We read about two dreams that Joseph had. One when he was among his brothers in the field binding sheaves, and his brothers' sheaves circle around his own and bow low to the ground. In the other dream, he sees the sun, moon, and eleven stars bowing down to him. These two dreams had similar meanings.

Pharoah also had two dreams that were similar. The difference between Joseph and Pharoah is that the great Joseph served the God of Israel, and Pharoah did not. God gave Joseph the interpretation of Pharoah's dream (Genesis 41).

Through the Bible, God spoke to his people and even to ungodly world leaders in dreams. King Nebuchadnezzar is one such world leader as well (Daniel 2). There is a skill in interpreting dreams and not everyone has that skill. As believers we need to pray and ask God to help us know the meaning of our dreams. Daniel went to the Lord to undertstand the dream of King Nebuchadnezzar. It is also important to know when you should ponder the dream and seek God, and rather than telling your dreams to just anyone tell those who are of the same spiritual mindset (Daniel 2:17-20 NLT).

God gave Daniel the interpretation of King Nebuchadnezzar's dream, and to Joseph the interpretation of Pharoah's dream. To draw a parallel, Reverend Brenda's two-in-one dream is as well. It is vital to understand that God and dreams did not end when the Bible closed. He continues to visit us in dreams, and with the help of the Holy Spirit, those dreams can be de-mystified and interpreted.

There is a clear message in Reverend Brenda's dream: the presence of God despite her disappointment. The beauty of her personal Psalm is her Love for God and how He has delivered her from difficult situations. Rev. Brenda's story shows how God's eye is upon us, and He knows what we feel inside even when we think He did not see or has forgotten.

As believers, we should be honored to be in the presence of the Lord and under His watchful eyes, regardless of whether He gives us what we want. I am reminded of Hagar. When Hagar was treated harshly by Sarai and evicted from the home, being pregnant with a son, God had His eyes on her. Being at her wit's end and not knowing what to do next, God sent an angel with a message and instructions. But we read in Genesis 16 that the message was that of deliverance, provision, blessings, and triumph. Hagar was astounded and said, "You are the God who sees me."

And she called the name of the Lord that spake unto her, Thou God seest me: for she said, Have I also here looked after him that seeth me? Wherefore the well was called Beerlahairoi; behold, it is between Kadesh and Bered (Genesis 16:14-15).

So dear reader, even when you think that God does not see you or know your longings or your dilemma, rest assured He does, and He knows what's best for us and when to release certain blessings to us. We need to rest confidently in His presence, knowing He will not withhold any good gifts.

For the LORD God is a sun and shield: the LORD will give grace and glory: no good thing will he withhold from them that walk uprightly (Psalm 84:11).

Pamela Rasheed

CHAPTER 17

Patricia White Backstory

My Psalm centers around the healing, deliverance, and miracle that was manifested in my brother Roger's life. Despite struggling with alcoholism for more than two decades as he journeyed through life, my brother has now experienced a transformation. The devil took him very low and down. At one time in his life, across the street from where he lived in the Caribbean country, Antigua. My brother used to harvest, and still harvest, sugarcane. At one point, he became overwhelmed with fear and retreated to live in a field for approximately two weeks. During this time, he was in hiding from others and remained undiscovered. While we were praying for my nephew, another woman was also praying for my brother's well-being. It was during this prayerful moment that my brother emerged from his hiding spot in the field. I inquired about his whereabouts and when he had exited the field, only to realize that it was the exact same hour that we were fervently praying. We thank God for that. He looked terrible and wild. However, we believe God was watching over him and delivered him from the wilderness and the wildness he had encountered during those two weeks of isolation. For this, we are incredibly grateful to God.

Despite his harrowing experience in the field, my brother's struggles with alcoholism persisted. However, there was a glimmer of hope when his boss at his government job got him into a rehabilitation program. Unfortunately, my brother did not take advantage of this opportunity for help. We continued to pray for him, and eventually, God granted him a breakthrough, and he decided to go the rehab to get the help he needed. In the beginning, he became overwhelmed as there were a lot of phone calls, but again, we kept on praying. Two days before he left, he called me, and after we spoke a few times over the day, he called again and said, "Pat, I am blind, I can't see." He lost his sight for about 5-10 minutes.

When he said that, I knew this was God. I said, "Roger, you need to listen to me." I uttered a prayer as the Holy Spirit gave it, and after praying, I asked, "How are your eyes?". He screamed and said, "It's blurry, it's blurry!" As we continued to pray, his sight returned. The next day he left for rehab and was there for about 1.5 years. God delivered him, and he has been living on his own and clean for over two years going on three.

I thank God for restoring his sight. I thank God for delivering him and for removing the fear and doubt. I praise God for who Roger is and who He is created to be today.

This is my story and testimony.

God is the deliverer and the healer of my brother. God makes beauty from ashes.

Patricia White's Psalm

God Answered My Prayer And Set My Brother Free

My Lord, My Savior, My God
You always hear me when I call.
In my devastation,
you calmed my hurt
and had compassion on me

You heard my cry a
And collected my tears
While there was no hope but thee.
The hurt of not knowing was a struggle for me
But my faith in You sustained me.

Deliverance Lord,
Deliverance Lord, set him free
As I remembered Your Word in John 14
You took away the trouble in my heart.
You set my brother free!

I believe, I believe

You restored the blinded eyes.
The Power of You, God!
The Power of my Prayer
The Power of Your Healing!
Hallelujah! Selah

Author's Exhortation

Mary, the mother of Jesus, played a pivotal role in a breakthrough when she stood in the gap of intercession between the host and Jesus at the wedding in Cana of Galilee.

There was a crisis that needed immediate intervention.

Jewish weddings were very steep in tradition in terms of their lavish customs, one of having the best wine and food in abundance. However, at this wedding, the wine ran out. Imagine the potential embarrassment! If food and wine run out at such an event, even in today's custom across cultures, it would bring great shame to the bride and bridegroom and their families.

Jesus and his disciples were present at the wedding in Cana. This story is recorded in John's gospel, chapter 2:1-1. His mother came to Him and said, "They have no more wine." In other words, she hopes that Jesus can tune the situation around. Although it seemed that Jesus brushed her off, she instructed the servants to "do whatever He says." The miracle of Jesus' turning water into wine was a game changer; not only did He turn water into the best wine, but He took away the shame that would have befallen the host of the wedding celebration.

It was with ease and confident trust that Mary presented the dilemma to Jesus while she beseeched the servants to follow directions. Mary's relationship with Jesus emboldened her. She knew who Jesus was and that He was a miracle worker, although this is recorded as His first miracle.

Dear readers, we are all like Mary. We must stand in the gap for others and say to Jesus, "They ran out of wine and will soon be left ashamed; please help them – give them the miracle of salvation, healing, and deliverance." He is the miracle worker and is waiting to turn water into wine in every situation. This was the first miracle that Jesus performed, and it can be the first miracle that your loved one can experience when you stand in the gap and intercede.

Sister Pat's relationship with Jesus allowed her to stand confidently in the gap of intercession at the time of the crisis that involved her brother. She, like Mary, said, "Jesus, my brother ran out of wine, help him!" while she instructed her to bother what to do, and he was healed, delivered, and set free.

Pamela Rasheed

CHAPTER 18
Sister Roshini's backstory

Betrayed a second time, I was devastated.

A range of emotions anger, rejection, betrayal, loneliness, and feeling of abandonment, not only by the earthly one but also by the Lord. At that time, I felt that God allowed me to go through the sting of rejection yet again. I became rebellious to the Lord fleetingly but relented just as quickly.

Finally, as I was in total desperation, amidst much weeping and repetitive groanings, I cried out to God. Months later, He rescued me by bringing me into a realm of Worship where I experienced His Presence and Infinite love. From this experience, I wrote this Psalm.

RAVELLED

Like rays of an afternoon sun
Giving out its most brilliant light
You wrapped me.
The intensity of Your fire on me
Left no room for the coldness of
the enemy's frigid visits.

Days ran into weeks, then flowed into months,
And stretched into years.
Weeping, moaning, groaning,
And despairing as to where I was.
Will it ever end?
Would there ever be days of peace
and bouts of laughter?

Gently calling and so softly
Whispering my name
He caught my attention as
His Holy Spirit wooed me to Him.
Hopelessly disinterested, I slowly and reluctantly
Started to gravitate to Him.

Now, like a soft blanket on a wintry day,
Oh! He made His Presence gloriously known to me.
Now, never the same again,
Oh no! I'll never ever be the same again.
Immersed in Him, now exclusively His.
He is my BELOVED, and I am HIS..

Author's Exhortation

Oh, that bitter sting of rejection! "It is so hard to bear," says anyone who has ever been rejected. But oh, how much more it must feel to go through such pain, yet a second time. Spurned, turned down, embarrassed, and feeling unworthy are the brick and mortar that create a deep dark cave where you feel like hiding for the rest of your life. And when you show your face as you must, a mask or façade is all people see until you enter that dark cave again.

The eighty-eight Psalm of the Holy Bible is known as the darkest and saddest Psalm ever written. While most Psalms that start with a burden or trouble reach a turning point where prayer, reflection, and faith have brought a ray of light and hope, Psalm 88 is the exception.

This Psalmist opened with these words, *"O LORD, God of my salvation, I have cried out day and night before You. Let my prayer come before You; Incline Your ear to my cry. My soul is full of troubles. And my life draws near to the grave."* (vv 1-3) and ends with *"Loved one and friend You have put far from me, And my acquaintances into darkness"* (v 18) In these eighteen verses the only positive statement that gives a ray of hope is that God is his salvation, and he is sure of that. Besides that, it is all a torrential rain of dejection, despair, depression, and death.

It is easy to become so bitter that you no longer want to pray, read your bible, or even feel joy in the things you once enjoyed. When you feel the pain from the sting and embarrassment of rejection as believers, God's love and power become elusive. This was certainly true of this psalmist when he said, *"O LORD, why do you cast my soul away? Why do you hide your face from me?"* (Ps. 88:14).

There is no doubt a thin line of knowing if this is the God is Salvation or the cause of the pain and troubles. But it is in this phase that it is vital to reassure yourself and know to whom you ultimately belong and who is He that matters after all. His name is Jesus, and He is the only one who would take you to Himself because He bore the cost of our rejection.

Psalm 88 is a depiction of Jesus himself. He stepped into that state of rejection, pain, darkness, and embarrassment on the cross of Calvary. He was the spotless lamb of God that knew no sin, yet He was beaten, spat upon, mocked, dragged through the streets, and down the road to Calvary, carrying the cross we should have carried. He, the Son of God, took our rejection, embarrassment, and sting of rejection openly. Oh, we owe Him Praise forever.

Jesus bore the sting of our rejection and died the death we deserve to assure us of God's complete forgiveness and unfailing love. Can you imagine that level of rejection, pain, tears, and embarrassment? Do you think you can face a fraction of it? Jesus took our place because of LOVE. Queen Elizabeth said, "Grief is the price we pay for Love."

So dear reader, when you feel rejected, allow yourself to reflect on Jesus. And like sister Roshinie, turn to worship and let the Holy Spirit polish you so you can become a crown jewel for His admiration! I'd rather be admired and loved by the one who bore my rejection sting, shame, despair, and death on His way to Calvary than any earthy one who can reject me. He took my place of rejection and grief, and I worship Him alone.

He is despised and rejected of men;
a man of sorrows, and acquainted with grief:
and we hid as it were our faces from him;
he was despised, and we esteemed him not.
Surely he hath borne our griefs, and carried our sorrows:
yet we did esteem him stricken, smitten of God, and afflicted.
But he was wounded for our transgressions,
he was bruised for our iniquities:
the chastisement of our peace was upon him;
and with his stripes we are healed.

(Isaiah 53:3-5)

Consider Writing a Review

When you enjoy a book, it is a natural desire to tell others about it. Amazon.com provides a way to share your thoughts and I invite you to write a book review. It is easy. Here are tips:

1. After going to the link below on Amazon.com, the first thing you are asked to do is to **assign a number of stars** to the book that matches your opinion of the book.

2. Create a **title** for the review. This can be a simple phrase, like "Awesome book." If you are not sure what to say, look at the titles of other book reviews.

3. It is easiest to write the book in a **word processor** and then paste it into Amazon.com. Your word processor will pick up typos before your review goes public.

4. Write the review as if you were **talking to another person** – you are – a person who comes to Amazon.com and is considering buying this book.

5. Include a description of what you found **most helpful**. Was it an idea, chapter, tip? Share that with the readers.

6. Next you may want to write **who you think would most benefit** from this book. Is it for a believer or someone else who is going through a difficult time and can benefit from this book? Or is it more appropriate for some - one with experience with this topic?

7. What if you have something **negative** to say about the book? You may always reach me at prasheed1@icloud.com to suggest changes in the book.

8. If you include negative feedback in the review, keep a positive perspective rather than attack me or any of the co-authors.

Here are some sample phrases:

- While overall the book was good, I would change it by...
- I don't think this book is right for...
- I would improve this book by...

Before you hit save, **read everything over one more time.** Authors and readers appreciate book reviews and they get easier to write with time. Go to this link on Amazon.com to write your review.

Also please email me at prasheed1@icloud.com when you have posted your review.

Thank you,

Pamela Rasheed